Watchman's Guide to the Time of the End

The Time is not near, it's here!

Christ said,

Be on your guard. I have told you everything ahead of time.

Mark 13:23

Richard H. Perry

Watchman's Guide to the Time of the End

Copyright © 2012, Richard H. Perry

Richard H Perry

Website: www.lastdaysmystery.info

Email: lastdaysmystery@yahoo.com

Youtube: www.youtube.com/user/richardperry2

Twitter: richardperry2

Table of Contents:

About the Author   4

Introduction   5

Chapter 1:   The Watchman   8

Chapter 2:   About Times and Dates   18

Chapter 3:   Four Horsemen of the Apocalypse   32

Chapter 4:   Rider on the White Horse   42

Chapter 5:   Rider on the Red Horse   59

Chapter 6:   End Time Babylonians   72

Chapter 7:   Rider on the Black Horse   82

Chapter 8:   Rider on the Pale Horse   111

Chapter 9:   Seven Trumpets   123

Chapter 10:   Second Coming   142

Chapter 11:   End Time Religion   168

Glossary   187

Other Books   197

About the Author

Richard has written several books which are listed on the last page of this book. He has appeared on History Channel's Nostradamus Effect: The Rapture.

He speaks and conducts prophecy conferences on the Time of the End and the Second Coming.

Richard has studied the Bible for over thirty years with a particular focus on the Time of the End and the Second Coming of the Messiah, called the Christ. Since 9/11 Yahweh has led Richard to rely on Scripture and the Spirit to help Yahweh's people to better understand what Yahweh expects. What He expects them to know and what He expects them to do.

In the past he has served as church elder; Vice-President of a local Full Gospel Businessmen's Fellowship International and taught Bible studies on the Time of the End to diverse groups both inside and outside the organized church.

During much of his business career he has held leadership positions in the corporate world. He also served for ten years with Habitat for Humanity International, including six years in Central America and then as Area Director for Latin America and the Caribbean.

He has studied at Elim Bible Institute and holds Bachelor of Science degree from Rochester Institute of Technology. Richard currently resides in North Georgia.

Introduction

For almost two thousand years Christians have been trying to understand about the "Time of the End" and when Jesus Christ would return to gather His people and establish the Kingdom of God on Earth. For even longer the Jewish people have been waiting for the Messiah to appear and restore the Kingdom to Israel as God promised.

These Christian and Jewish beliefs about the "Time of the End" have captured the imagination of the whole world which is obsessed with the idea of the End of the World.

Over the centuries so many books have been written about the End that the actual Bible prophesies have become obscured by popular terminology and the teachings of Man. These popular teachings have so confused and obscured the biblical message that now even the Christians and Jews themselves have lost much of the truth as presented in Scripture.

The Scripture is true, all of it, and that is what this book will proclaim about the biblical "Time of the End." You may already believe that Scripture is true, but how can you be sure that my presentation of it will be true?

First, and most importantly, you cannot trust me or any Man for the Truth. You must seek it directly from Almighty God through His Word and His Spirit. This is your personal responsibility and you should not delegate it to anyone else.

With that said, this is why you should keep reading. As I present the "Time of the End" to you I will show you key passages of Scripture from which I derive my point of view. This will make it easy for you to follow and enable you to consider what I am presenting when you do your own Bible reading.

Also, I will attempt to follow the biblical instructions for properly handling the Word of God. For example, I will use Scripture to interpret Scripture. This is like letting God explain what He is talking about.

For example here is how the Word of God says this, "Do not go beyond what is written." Then you will not take pride in one man over against another" (1 Corinthians 4:6).

The ideas I present will be in context with the passages, the book referenced and the whole of the Scriptural message.

I have been diligently reading and studying the Bible for over thirty years. I have consulted over 180 other books regarding the "Time of the End" and the "Second Coming" of Christ. But, in the last ten years the Lord has directed me to rely on Him only and to trust Him completely regarding what He is saying. This began as a difficult process of setting aside false ideas I had believed to be true because of what I had been taught by Man. However, as I encountered one error in teaching, it led to another and then to another and into several deceptive traditions of Men which had crept into the religious institutions. Finally, I learned to rely on the Word of God and His Spirit, and what I learned I will share with you in this book.

Be of an open mind to accept the Word of God as lead by the Spirit of God and do not follow the teachings and traditions of Man.

"This is what the LORD (Yahweh) says: 'Cursed is the one who trusts in man, who depends on flesh for his strength and whose heart turns away from Yahweh. ... 'But blessed is the man who trusts in Yahweh, whose confidence is in him" (Jeremiah 17:5, 7).

There is another reason to consider what is being presented in this interpretation of God's Word about the "Time of the End." God said that His Word regarding the "Time of the End" would be closed and sealed" until Now. He said this most clearly in the last chapter of Daniel, as we read here, "Go your way, Daniel, because the words are closed up and sealed until the time of the end" (Daniel 12:9).

Now, I will show you from Scripture and tell you how I know that the **"Time of the End has Come."**

Chapter 1
The Watchman

The title of this book is "Watchman's Guide to the Time of the End". The title makes a bold claim. It indicates that topic of the Time of the End is being presented by a Watchman. What is a Watchman?

Over the centuries there have been hundreds of books written about the coming end of the age and the return of the Messiah, called Christ. These books have been written by all kinds of people; academic scholars, scientists, pastors, evangelists, eschatological enthusiasts, so called prophets and apostles. Many of their works are known to us. However, when it comes to anticipating what would happen at the End of the Age leading up to Christ's return, they have been found wanting.

Therefore, many have undertaken the role of a Watchman. But, who are the Watchmen of Yahweh, Almighty God? For the answer, let's consult Scripture regarding the Watchman of Yahweh?

I am going to present some Scripture for your consideration. This will be like a mini Bible Study on the Watchman. Here is what Yahweh has to say.

Who is the true Watchman?

Yahweh, the God of the Bible, is the true Watchman. Unless God Himself is watching out for His people, His people will not know what is coming.

> "Unless the LORD (Yahweh) watches over the city,
> the watchmen stand guard in vain." (Psalm 127:1)

The Watchman has been called by Yahweh.

> "Son of man, I have made you a watchman for the house of Israel; so hear the word I speak and give them warning from me." Ezekiel 33:7

The Watchman hears from God.

A Watchman has the Spirit of Yahweh, is a man of faith, earnestly seeks and hears from Yahweh.

> "He who belongs to God hears what God says." (John 8:47)

The Watchman is taught by God.

Many people are taught by Man, but the Watchman of Yahweh is taught by God.

> "All this I have spoken while still with you. But the Counselor, the Holy Spirit, whom the Father will send in my name, will teach you all things and will remind you of everything I have said to you." (John 8:25-26)

The Watchman understands God's Word.

The God of the Bible is **not** hard to understand. He is the best communicator in the universe; no one is better. Here is what God says to His people about His Word:

> "For we do not write you anything you cannot read or understand." (2 Corinthians 1:13)

The Watchman does not follow Man.

Many teachers and shepherds in the household of God are followers of the teachings and traditions of Men, men learn from men. Yahweh warned us against men like these.

> Yahweh, 'I am against **the prophets who steal from one another words** supposedly from me." (Jeremiah 23:30)

Christ spoke harshly against religious leaders like these and warned the people to leave them. Christ said,

"Thus you nullify the word of God for the sake of your tradition. ... They worship me in vain; **their teachings are but rules taught by men**. Jesus called the crowd to him and said ... **Leave them**; they are blind guides. If a blind man leads a blind man, both will fall into a pit." (Matthew 15:7-14)

The Watchman warns of the coming War.

"But if **the watchman sees the sword coming** and does not blow the trumpet to warn the people and the sword comes and takes the life of one of them, that man will be taken away because of his sin, but **I will hold the watchman accountable** for his blood" (Ezekiel 33:6).

The Watchman warns people to repent.

"Son of man, I have made you a watchman for the house of Israel; so hear the word I speak and **give them warning from me**. When I say to the wicked, 'O wicked man, you will surely die,' and you do not speak out to **dissuade him from his ways, that wicked man will die** for his sin, and I will hold you accountable for his blood. But if you do warn the wicked man to turn from his ways and he does not do so, **he will die for his sin, but you will have saved yourself**" (Ezekiel 33:7-9).

The Watchman prepares the way for the Messiah.

"I tell you the truth, the man who does not enter the sheep pen by the gate, but climbs in by some other way, is a thief and a robber. The man who enters by the gate is the shepherd of his sheep. **The watchman opens the gate for him**, and the sheep listen to his voice" (John 10:1-3).

The Watchman finds hostility in God's household.

"The prophet, along with my God, is the watchman over Ephraim, yet snares await him on all his paths, and **hostility in the house of his God**" (Hosea 9:8).

Not many listen to the Watchman.

"**I appointed watchmen** over you and said, 'Listen to the sound of the trumpet!' But you said, **'We will not listen.'** Therefore hear, O nations; observe, O witnesses, what will happen to them. Hear, O earth: I am bringing disaster on this people, the fruit of their schemes, because **they have not listened to my words and have rejected my law**" (Jeremiah 6:17-19).

The Watchman is only human.

There have been a number of books, articles and youtube.com videos documenting what Yahweh has revealed to me over the years. With minor corrections for increased revelation, the messages in these works remain consistent with Scripture.

Of course, any work on prophecy must stand the test of time and that is what will distinguish this work from those of others. We have already entered into the Time of the End and the next prophecies to be fulfilled will be occurring within a very few years. Therefore, whether or not I have heard from Yahweh will be apparent.

Background

I grew up in a small town protestant church. When I went away to collage, I left the church. Shortly thereafter my father became 'Born Again' through the influence of the Full Gospel Businessmen's Fellowship International. He and my mother began to earnestly pray that I would receive Christ. Eight year later I was led to read the Book of Revelation.

Revelation so intrigued me that I ended up reading other books about Revelation. While these other books differed widely in their interpretation, they universally indicted that any correct understanding of Revelation could only be found by first understanding the earlier books of the Bible. I then began to read through the whole of Scripture from Genesis to Revelation. During this four month journey through the Word of God I accepted Christ for who He claimed to be a dedicated my life to Him.

After years in corporate management, He led me to ten years of foreign mission with Habitat for Humanity International. After Habitat I returned to corporate management until the Lord made it clear that He had other things for me to do.

Just after 9/11, at two in the morning the Lord woke me and told me to pray for the two classes I was teaching. As I was praying He told me to see Dr. Schaefer, a man I did not know at the time. The next morning I called the office of a U.G.A. professor named Dr. Henry 'Fritz' Scheafer and left a message. Later that afternoon he returned my call a suggested that we get together. When we meet and discussed the Second Coming of Christ he said that I was to write a book. I began writing that book in 2001 and published it in 2003. "Of the Last Days: Listen, I Tell You A Mystery" is a comprehensive biblical study on the timing of Christ's Second Coming and the resurrection gathering of His Church.

When the book was published I spent several months seeking the Lord and asking Him, "What am I to do with this book? Then one day He told me to take what He had given me and warn the pastors. Over the next several weeks I spoke with about 12 pastors who I knew and was aquatinted with. When none of them seemed the least bit interested, I stopped the assignment.

Several months later as I was reading the Prophet Ezekiel the Lord informed me that I had not finished my assignment. That was also first time He told me that I would be a Watchman for His people.

I immediately made a list of all the pastors in my area and a few others that I knew. With a list of 160 pastors, I began contacting and speaking with any of the pastors who would meet with me. I sent a follow up letter to each pastor I spoke with and sent the following letter to those who would not.

Pastor _____ :   From 2003 through 2005

Over the past several years the Lord has been giving me a message for His Church. About a year ago He told me to warn the pastors. Since the message is extremely important, I am sending it to you. If you would like to speak with me or know more please call. The message has three parts.

First - There is no Pre-Tribulation Rapture.

Below, Paul describes the Resurrection and Rapture of the Church.

> *According to the Lord's own word, we tell you that we who are still alive, who are left till the coming of the Lord, will certainly not precede those who have fallen asleep. For the Lord himself will* **come down from heaven**, *with a loud command, with the voice of the archangel and with the trumpet call of God, and the dead in Christ will rise first. After that, we who are still alive and are left will be caught up together with them in the clouds to meet the Lord in the air* (1 Thessalonians 4:15-17).

Notice, Paul states that Jesus will come down from heaven and the believers will meet Him in the air. Now read Acts 3:21.

> *He must* **remain in heaven until** *the time comes for God to restore everything, as he promised long ago through his holy prophets* (Acts 3:21).

God does not restore everything until after the Tribulation. Therefore, the Church is caught up after the Tribulation. This is just one of the Bible's many prophetic words which contradict the Pre-Tribulation Rapture myth.

Second - Now is the time to teach what the Bible says about the Second Coming.

A couple of years ago, as I was reading through the Olivet Discourse, this passage caught my attention.

> So you also must be ready, because the Son of Man will come at an hour when you do not expect him. "Who then is the faithful and wise servant, whom the master has put in charge of the servants in his household to **give them their food at the proper time**? (Matthew 24:44-45)

As I read the words "*at the proper time*," I heard in my mind's ear an emphatic – **NOW!** As I considered the meaning of NOW, I asked the Lord, are you saying you're coming soon? His answer was also emphatic – NO, **Now is the time to teach what Scripture says about My return, because your children and their children will need to know.**

Finally – It's critical we understand Christ's commands regarding the Second Coming.

After asking the Lord for months about the importance of His teachings on the Second Coming, He awoke me one morning from a sound sleep and told me to pray for a class I was teaching. As I prayed, He gave me this:

> They will dash you to the ground, you and the children within your walls. They will not leave one stone on another, **because** you did not recognize the time of God's coming to you (Luke 19:44)

> From everyone who has been given much, much will be demanded; and from the one who has been entrusted with much, much more will be asked (Luke 12:48).

As He gave me the first verse, the word **"because"** burned in my mind. When I received the second verse, I understood the answer to my question. The first verse takes place at the time of the First Coming of Christ. As Christ entered Jerusalem, He told the religious leaders that **because** they did not recognize the time of His First Coming, Jerusalem and the Temple were going to be destroyed. This happened in 70 AD and 1,100,000 people were killed (men, women and children).

While Jesus commanded Israel to know the time of His First Coming, He requires much more from His Church regarding His Second Coming, and the Word of God repeatedly tells us we must know and understand this. If the Christian Church does not wake up and keep watch, what do you think a righteous God will do?

In the grace and peace of Christ Jesus,

Richard H. Perry

I finished my assignment of warning the pastors in November of 2005. I had personally met with and warned 86 pastors. By November I had warned over 145 pastors one way or the other. As far as I could tell, none of the pastors have taken to heart the warning.

It was in that month, November 2005, that the Lord seemed to be telling me to finish my assignment because He had something else for me to do.

Then in that same month, Penguin Publishing contacted me and asked if I would write "The Complete Idiot's Guide to the Last Days". I agreed and wrote the book which Penguin released in November 2006.

In 2007 I was invited to Jerusalem, Israel in September for the Feast of Yahweh, called Sukkot (Feast of Tabernacles) and a TV interview on Frontline Israel. That same year I lost my job and the Lord said to me, "I have something else you need to do."

A few weeks later Dr. Gavin Finley, of endtimepilgrim.org, gave me some software for making videos. Gavin said that I needed to get my message out on Youtube and Godtube. On January 8th of 2008 I uploaded my first video to Youtube which was titled the "Four Horsemen of the Apocalypse". I now have over 500 teaching and current event videos on Youtube.

The year 2008 became a very eventful year with the Lord, one in which He taught me several things from Scripture and told me to write a book, "The Time of the End Has Come: Our Journey Begins". Also, during this year the Lord reiterated that I was to be a Watchman for His people. He said that I was not to hold anything back, even though His message would not be popular in the household of God.

Prior to 2008 the Lord had already been showing me in His Word that the Seals of Revelation were critical to understanding the beginning of the Time of the End. Then in 2008 He showed me that the "Parable of the Ten Virgins" of Matthew 25 was directly tied to the Second Seal prophecy of Revelation 6. This meant that the Church would finally awake from their deep sleep when the Red Horse and its rider took peace from the earth.

It was in 2009 that the Lord, Yahweh, spoke to me in the spirit and said, "The red horse symbolizes Iran. I have stirred up the kings of the Medes because my purpose is to destroy Babylon." This revelation was a clear indication to me that Iran and its leaders would be responsible for starting World War III.

Even though my last book "The Time of the End Has Come: Our Journey Begins" was to be for the Church **after** the Second Seal of Revelation was opened, I released a "First Seal Edition" titled "The Time Has Come: Our Journey Begins" in December 2011. The "Second Seal Edition" titled "The Time of the End Has Come: Our Journey Begins" will be released after the Second Seal, Yahweh willing.

Chapter 2
About Times and Dates

The apostle Paul once wrote this to the Church in Thessalonica.

> "Now, brothers, about times and dates we do not need to write to you, for you know very well that the day of the Lord will come like a thief in the night" (1 Thessalonians 5:1-2).

Never the less, Paul did write to the Church to help them understand and that is what I am doing in this book.

However, the "Time of the End" is not the only period of time referenced in Scripture. Therefore, in this chapter, I will cover the other time periods that will be helpful to our understanding of the "Time of the End." The other relevant time periods mentioned in Scripture are as follows:

1. This Age and the age to come.
2. The Last Days
3. The Time of the End a.k.a. End Time
4. The Great Tribulation
5. The Day of Yahweh a.k.a. the Day of the LORD

Note: Man has invented other time periods that are not found in Scripture like, a Church Age and a seven year Tribulation. We will only be discussing those times mentioned in Scripture.

1. This Age and the Age to Come

During Jesus' ministry He referred to two ages, this present age in which we now live and a second age which is to come in the future. Below are some of His teachings about the two ages:

> "Anyone who speaks a word against the Son of Man will be forgiven, but anyone who speaks against the Holy Spirit will not be forgiven, either in this age or in the age to come (Matthew 12:32).

"I tell you the truth,' Jesus said to them, 'no one who has left home or wife or brothers or parents or children for the sake of the kingdom of God will fail to receive many times as much in this age and, in the age to come, eternal life" (Luke 18:29, 30).

"Jesus replied, 'The people of this age marry and are given in marriage. But those who are considered worthy of taking part in that age and in the resurrection from the dead will neither marry nor be given in marriage, and they can no longer die; for they are like the angels. They are God's children, since they are children of the resurrection" (Luke 20:34-36).

This age, the one in which we now live, will continue until Christ returns and establishes His Kingdom on earth. That is the age all believers are waiting for. In Luke 20:34, Jesus tells us that those who are worthy to take part in "that age" will be called children of the resurrection.

Jesus referred to only two ages, "this age" and the "age to come." Some people speak about what they call a "Church Age." Nowhere in the Bible is a "Church Age" ever mentioned, it is something Man has made up to fit their new theology.

In this book I try to use biblical terms for biblical ideas to minimize confusion. Today, Man uses numerous man-made terms to explain what God is saying. As if God needed our help to say what He means. After all God is a better communicator to His people than anyone. That is one reason why the Word of God makes this warning.

"Do not go beyond what is written. Then you will not take pride in one man over against another" (1 Corinthians 4:6).

The Kingdom comes at the End of the Age

The Parable of the Wheat and Tares is one of several parables Jesus employed to tell us about the coming Kingdom of God. The Parable of the Wheat and Tares provides insight into how and when the Kingdom of God will come. Christ's disciples asked Him for an explanation of the parable and this is what He said,

> "The one who sowed the good seed is the Son of Man. **The field is the world,** and the good seed stands for the sons of the kingdom. The weeds are the sons of the evil one, and the enemy who sows them is the devil. **The harvest is the end of the age**, and **the harvesters are angels**. As the weeds are pulled up and burned in the fire, so it will be at the end of the age. The Son of Man will send out his angels, and they will weed out of his kingdom everything that causes sin and all who do evil. They will throw them into the fiery furnace, where there will be weeping and gnashing of teeth. Then the righteous will shine like the sun in the kingdom of their Father. He who has ears let him hear" (Matthew 13:37-43).

Jesus states, "The field is the world." and explains that the wheat symbolizes the righteous and the tares are the unrighteous, which must grow together until the "harvest" at "**the end of the age**." "The harvesters are the angels" who will separate the wheat from the tares at the "harvest."

The Parable of the Dragnet also describes the same thing. The righteous will be gathered and the wicked will be separated out for punishment. Here is how Christ told that parable.

> "Once again, the kingdom of heaven is like a net that was let down into the lake and caught all kinds of fish. When it was full, the fishermen pulled it up on the shore. Then they sat down and collected the good fish in baskets, but threw the bad away. This is how it will be **at the end of the age**. The angels will come and separate the wicked from the righteous and throw them into the fiery furnace, where there will be weeping and gnashing of teeth" (Matthew 13:47-50).

As we can see from history, an age is a long period of time. We are still in "this age" that Christ referred to because the "age to come," the Kingdom of God has not yet arrived.

Time of the End
This Age and the Age to Come

The "Time of the End" is at end of this age, just before the age to come. The age to come is when Christ returns and begins to reign in His kingdom on earth.

Scripture describes another time which also covers many generations.

2. The Last Days

The next period of time is what the Bible calls the "Last Days." For a comprehensive work on this topic see my second book, "The Complete Idiot's Guide to the Las Days." However, let's take a quick look at what Scripture says concerning the Last Days.

We first see the Last Days mentioned by the prophet Isaiah in context with the coming Kingdom of God on earth. Here is what Isaiah wrote:

> "In the **last days** the mountain of the Lord's temple will be established as chief among the mountains; it will be raised above the hills, and all nations will stream to it" (Isaiah 2:2).

This prophecy indicates that the Kingdom of God will be over all the nations in the Last Days. We should realize that the Kingdom of God does not come on earth until the Messiah, called Christ returns and takes His throne as King. Revelation 11:15 tells us that He will begin His reign when the seventh and last trumpet sounds. Revelation 20 indicates that His reign will be for a thousand years. Therefore, one of the Last Days encompasses what we call the Millennium.

Before we go any further we should be clear about what God means regarding a 'day' in the context of the 'Last Days.' First, the 24 hour day that we are all familiar with, is not the 'day' that God is referring to regarding the 'Last Days.' When God wants to specify a 24 hour days He will say it this way,

> "He said to me, "It will take 2,300 **evenings and mornings**; then the sanctuary will be reconsecrated" (Daniel 8:14).

This is the same way God spoke in the Genesis creation account.

> "And God said, "Let there be light," and there was light.... God called the light "day," and the darkness he called "night." And there was **evening, and there was morning-- the first day**" (Genesis 1:3-5).

However, when God speaks about the 'Last Days', He is not talking about 24 hour days. Here is what He says,

> "For a thousand years in your sight are like a day that has just gone by, or like a watch in the night" (Psalm 90:4).

> "But do not forget this one thing, dear friends: With the Lord a day is like a thousand years, and a thousand years are like a day" (2 Peter 3:8).

Therefore, when it comes to the 'Last Days', God is referring to days that are a thousand years like the thousand year reign of Christ - Revelation 20:4 "They came to life and reigned with Christ a thousand years."

In the book of Hebrews we are told that the Sabbath Rest for the people of God will be the Seventh Day.

> "There remains, then, a [seventh day] Sabbath-rest for the people of God" (Hebrews 4:9).

The 'Last Days' ends with the seventh day Millennial reign of Christ. When did the Last Days begin? Once again, the book of Hebrews has the answer.

> "In the past God spoke to our forefathers through the prophets at many times and in various ways, but **in these last days** he has spoken to us by his Son" (Hebrews 1:1-2).

The Last Days began when Christ was speaking which was during His First Coming, two thousand years ago. Two thousand years with the Lord are like two days.

Therefore, the Millennium is the seventh day (Day 7) and it is in the future.

Christ was speaking in the Last Days which was two thousand years ago. So, Christ was speaking at the beginning of Day 5. Let me show you in the chart below how I have come to understand the 7 days of God, including the Last Days (Day 5, Day 6 and Day 7). The biblical Last Days are shown in black.

The Last Days and End Time

Day 1	Day 2	Day 3	Day 4	Day 5	Day 6	Day 7
1,000	2,000	3,000	4,000	5,000	6,000	7,000
Adam	Noah	Moses	David	Christ 32 AD	E T 2012	Sabbath Rest

The chart above shows biblical history from Adam and creation through the Millennium (Day 7). From Adam to the Messiah was four thousand years. From the Messiah in 32 A.D. to 2012 is 1,980 years, almost two days. Therefore, we are currently at the very end of six thousand years, or six days. There remains then a Sabbath Rest of one thousand years. The Millennium when the Messiah will reign on earth.

With the chart above in mind, we can see that the "Last Days" to God would include Day 5 - when Christ was speaking, Day 6 – present day and Day 7 - the Millennium.

The "Time of the End" in context of the Last Days comes at the very end of Day 6, just before Day 7.

So far we have been leading up to the Time of the End. Now we will discuss the main topic of the book.

3. The Time of the End

The first place in Scripture that we read about the "Time of the End" is in the book of Daniel. Daniel as we know received many prophecies from God concerning the "Time of the End." The prophecies of Daniel are critical to understanding the Time of the End. Christ specifically told His followers in Matthew 24:15 that they are to understand what Daniel wrote.

The prophecies that Daniel received from God about the Time of the End are recorded in chapters 2, 7, 8, 9, 11 and 12. Daniel was told,

> "Son of man, understand that the vision concerns **the time of the end**. ... I am going to tell you what will happen later in the time of wrath, because the vision concerns **the appointed time of the end**" (Daniel 8:17, 19).

Daniel was also told something that is very important to our study of the "Time of the End." Daniel was told,

"Go your way, Daniel, because the words are **closed up and sealed <u>until</u> the time of the end**" (Daniel 12:9).

What does this mean that the words are closed and sealed, since we can plainly see and read God's words to Daniel as well as the other prophets? As usual, God's words mean what they say. Therefore, there was no way that anyone could have correctly understood God's words before the "Time of the End" when God's words would be unsealed and opened.

It also appears that God was giving us a clue when He said "**closed up and sealed**." Because, we now know that the Seals of Revelation are key to correctly understanding the "Time of the End." We will also learn in our study that there was no way anyone would be able to understand about the Time of the End **until** the Seals of Revelation began to be opened. We will discuss this in detail in the next chapter. For now here is a chart showing that the seven seals span the Time of the End.

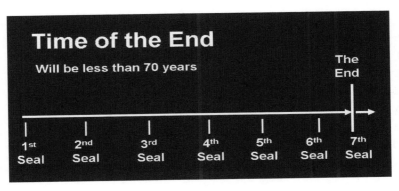

What else have we been told about the End Time?

Christ told us many things about the time which leads to the End of the age. He told us when the Time of the End would begin and about how long it would last.

At the time of Christ's First Coming, just a few days before He made His sacrifice on the cross, Christ's disciples asked Him for a sign of His Second Coming and the end of the age. Below Christ tells them when that time would begin. Christ said,

> "Nation will rise against nation, and kingdom against kingdom. There will be famines and earthquakes in various places. **All these are the beginning** of birth pains" (Matthew 24:7-8).

When ever I quote this verse to people, I almost always get the same response. They say something like this. "But, all these things have been happening since there have been nations. So, how can we be certain when the Time of the End will begin?"

First, I remind them of what Christ said in Mark 13:23. When Christ was telling His disciples about the Time of the End, He said, "Be on your guard. **I have told you everything ahead of time.**"

Since Christ has already told us everything ahead of time, we can be certain that somewhere in Scripture He already told us what we need to know in order to determine when the Time of the End begins.

Because, we are unable to determine a start time using only the Matthew 24 passage "**All these are the beginning.**" Therefore, this passage must be pointing us to something else God has told us about the End Time. Is there any place else in Scripture that includes all the things that Christ said would mark the beginning of birth pains? Yes, there is one other place in prophecy that includes all these things: wars, famines, pestilences and earthquakes. That one place is the Seals of Revelation chapter six. Therefore, it must be the Seals that contain the specific prophecies we need to determine when the Time of the End begins.

In the next several chapters of this book I will be showing from Scripture how we can now know for certain that the Seals of Revelation are the keys to understanding the Time of the End.

We now have a good biblical perspective of where the "Time of the End" fits into "this age" and in the "Last Days." Next we need to understand about what Christ called the "Great Tribulation."

4. The Great Tribulation

It was Christ that called this time period the "Great Tribulation" in Matthew 24. He was telling His disciples what would happen immediately following the "abomination that causes desolation" when He described the "Great Tribulation."

> "There will be **great tribulation,** unequaled from the beginning of the world until now--and never to be equaled again" (Matthew 24:21).

When He was describing the Great Tribulation He used words very similar to the words He had given Daniel when He was describing this time of unparalleled tribulation. Here is what He said to Daniel, so we can see the similarity.

> "At that time Michael, the great prince who protects your people, will arise. There will be a time of **tribulation** such as has not happened from the beginning of nations until then. But at that time your people--everyone whose name is found written in the book--will be delivered" Daniel 12:1).

It is also from Daniel that we first learn how long the Great Tribulation will last. Remember that Christ indicated the Great Tribulation begins with the "abomination that causes desolation." We can tell from Daniel 9 that this tribulation will be exactly three and a half years. Let's look at the prophecy in Daniel that gives us this information.

> "He [Antichrist] will confirm a covenant with many for one 'seven.' **In the middle of the 'seven'** he will put an end to sacrifice and offering. And on a wing of the temple **he will set up an abomination that causes desolation**, until the end that is decreed is poured out on him" (Daniel 9:27).

As we can see in this verse half way through the last seven (3 ½ years) the Antichrist sets up the "abomination that causes desolation." The book of Revelation in chapter 12 also confirms this period of time when it tells us when Michael the great prince throws Satan from heaven to earth. More on that in chapter 9: Seven Trumpets, when we discuss the Great Tribulation in detail.

Now, let's take a look at the "Time of the End" timeline with the "Great Tribulation" inserted where it will occur.

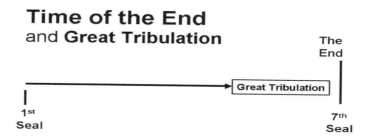

After the Great Tribulation the Messiah, called Christ, will return when the last trumpet sounds and establish His Kingdom on earth as we are told in Revelation chapter 15 as we read below:

> "The seventh angel sounded his trumpet, and there were loud voices in heaven, which said: "**The kingdom of the world has become the kingdom of our Lord and of his Christ**, and he will reign for ever and ever" (Revelation 11:15).

The Messiah returns after the Great Tribulation, just as He said He would in Matthew 24:29-30.

> "Immediately **after the tribulation** of those days … They will see the Son of Man coming on the clouds of the sky, with power and great glory" (Matthew 24:29-30).

The next period of time that we will discuss takes place after the Time of the End when the Messiah returns. The Messiah returns on the "Day of Yahweh" also known as the "Day of the Lord."

5. The Day of the LORD

The Day of the LORD is the most documented period of time in biblical prophecy. It is referred to, so often, that both the Old and New Testament prophets often just refer to it as "that day" or "the day."

In this chapter I will only be showing you some of the basics regarding the Day of the LORD. But we will cover this important topic in more detail in chapter 10, The Second Coming.

Highlights of the Day of the LORD:

These are some of the major events that will take place when the Day of the LORD arrives, as stated in the Word of God.

The Messiah returns.

> **"The LORD thunders at the head of his army**; his forces are beyond number, and mighty are those who obey his command. The day of Yahweh (the LORD) is great; it is dreadful. Who can endure it?" (Joel 2:11)

His followers are gathered.

> "The sun will be turned to darkness and the moon to blood before the coming of the great and dreadful day of the LORD. And everyone who calls on the name of Yahweh will be saved; for on Mount Zion and in Jerusalem **there will be deliverance**, as Yahweh has said, **among the survivors whom Yahweh calls**" (Joel 2:31-32).

The Kingdom of God on earth is established.

"On **'that day'** living water will flow out from Jerusalem, half to the eastern sea and half to the western sea, in summer and in winter. The LORD will be king over the whole earth. On that day there will be one Yahweh, and his name the only name" (Zechariah 14:8-9).

Judgment Day

"The day of the LORD is near for all nations. **As you have done, it will be done to you**; your deeds will return upon your own head" (Obadiah 1:15).

God's wrath on the wicked is poured out.

"See, the day of Yahweh (the LORD) is coming --**a cruel day, with wrath and fierce anger**-- to make the land desolate and destroy the sinners within it" (Isaiah 13:9).

The new heaven and new earth come.

"But the day of the Lord will come like a thief. The heavens will disappear with a roar; the elements will be destroyed by fire, and the earth and everything in it will be laid bare. ... That day will bring about the destruction of the heavens by fire, and the elements will melt in the heat" (2 Peter 3:10, 12).

Below are the End Time and the Day of the LORD presented in a timeline.

Time of the End and
The Day of the LORD

The apostle Paul said that the Day of the Lord would catch the world by surprise – but not those in Christ. The brothers in Christ he said would NOT be surprised by "that day." Here is what Paul wrote,

> "Now, brothers, <u>about times and dates</u> we do not need to write to you, for you know very well that **the day of the Lord** will come like a thief in the night. While people are saying, "Peace and safety," destruction will come on them suddenly, as labor pains on a pregnant woman, and they will not escape. **But you, brothers, are not in darkness so that this day should surprise you like a thief**" (1 Thessalonians 5:1-4).

We now know about:
- This Age and the age to come.
- The Last Days
- The Time of the End
- The Great Tribulation
- The Day of the LORD

Chapter 3
Four Horsemen of the Apocalypse

The book of Revelation contains three series of prophecies that describe major events related to the Time of the End; seven seals, seven trumpets and seven bowls. Each of these seal, trumpet and bowl prophecies will mark major events that will be taking place during the Time of the End and the return of Christ. We will be discussing each of these prophecies as we go through this book.

The first series of End Time prophecies are the seven seals. The seven seals span the Time of the End from its beginning, to the end of the age and Christ's return.

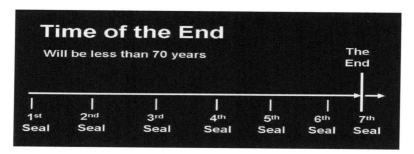

The first four seals of Revelation are the early warning signs of the Time of the End. The first four prophecies describe specific historical events that will occur as the Time of the End begins. As of January 31, 2012, only the first seal of Revelation has been opened and fulfilled. When Christ opened the first seal, events began to take place that changed the world and ushered it into the Time of the End. I will be explaining the first seal prophecy and its fulfillment in chapter 4, Rider on the White Horse.

There are a couple of important aspects to these End Time prophecies that I should point out to you before we continue. The Bible describes these early warning signs as "birth pains."

"Terror will seize them, pain and anguish will grip them; they will writhe like a woman in labor. They will look aghast at each other, their faces aflame. See, the day of the LORD [Yahweh] is coming" (Isaiah 13:8-9).

"Nation will rise against nation, and kingdom against kingdom. There will be famines and earthquakes in various places. All these are the beginning of birth pains' (Matthew 24:7-8).

What do we know about birth pains?

Birth Pains: Severity

One of the reasons that God calls these signs "birth pains" is because they will be progressive in the same way that birth pains are progressive. As birth pains increase in severity, so will the seal prophecies increase in severity as they progresses toward the coming kingdom. Therefore, we can expect that the Second Seal prophecy will be larger than the first and so forth through the End Time.

Birth Pains: Frequency

Birth pains also occur closer and closer together as delivery approaches. This means that the number of years between the first and second seal prophecies will be greater than the number of years between second and third seal prophecies and so forth.

The second seal prophecy will be the next major End Time biblical prophecy to be fulfilled. Just as in birth pains; the fulfillment of the Second Seal prophecy will be more severe than the First. I will discuss the Second Seal prophecy in chapter 5, Rider on the Red Horse.

But, first I should explain how I receive the revelation about Scripture and Bible prophecy. Much of what I now believe, I did not hear or read from any Man. For the most part, what I now believe I have received from Yahweh in His Word as taught by His Spirit. Many of my previous beliefs, what we call paradigms, I've set aside in favor of what I read in Scripture and hear from the Holy Spirit.

Let me tell you a little about how this has happened to me.

Yahweh shows me.

By 2001 I had been a serious student of Scripture for over 20 years. However, it was about 2001 when the Lord, Yahweh, began showing me how to submit to Him and rely on His Word. While I was writing "Of The Last Days: Listen, I Tell You A Mystery" I researched over 180 commentaries and eschatological works on the topics of; the Last Days, the Time of the End and the Second Coming. These works had been written from as early as 1733 to present day by the leading Christian scholars of their time. These works contained both popular and academic writings about Bible Prophecy. They presented an incredible divergence of opinion about what God was saying in prophecy. It became apparent that if I was to write a clear and accurate picture of the Second Coming – I could not rely on the ideas of Man to guide me. So, I set all these books aside and began to submit myself to Scripture in order to see what Yahweh had to say about the Second Coming.

After years of serious biblical study, I thought that I knew something about the Bible. However, as I look back now, I can see that I knew more about what "**Man said God said**" than I knew for myself "**what Yahweh Himself said.**" As this realization began to sink in, I began to change my thinking. Little by little I relied less and less on the teachings of Man and more and more on Yahweh's Word. The more I relied on Scripture the more the Holy Spirit showed me. This process continues to this day and it has opened His Word in a way that challenges almost everything I had previously been taught.

Let me show you a few fundamental truths that Yahweh has revealed to me from His Word.

All too often when I ask people if they read their Bible, I get this response; "Not as often as I should." To which I ask, "Why is that?" Usually they say, "I don't understand what the Bible is saying." This of course is a very sad state of affairs for God's people. There are several reasons that this is true today and I have to admit that this was part of my problem as well. That's why I initially consulted commentaries and other Christian writings as I tried to understand the Bible about the Second Coming.

Then one day the Lord pointed out to me a word from Scripture that challenged and encouraged me. Here is what the Lord said to me about His Word:

> "We do not write you anything you cannot read or understand" (2 Corinthians 1:13).

This meant that there is nothing in the Word of God that I cannot read and understand. Of course this word is not just for me. This word is for all of God's people. There are, however, prerequisites like; having the Holy Spirit, seeking God in truth and regular work at correctly handling the Word.

While other seekers may be helpful to me as I search for truth, I must not rely on them. I am to trust and rely on Yahweh alone. After all, can there be a better communicator for the people of God than Yahweh Himself? No! Therefore, if you have the Spirit of God, you too can read and understand the Word of God. Trust Him to tell you what you need to know.

As I began to rely more and more on the Word of God for the truth, He showed me Scripture to reinforce and encourage my resolve. Here are a couple of passages I find very helpful.

> **"Every word of God is flawless**; he is a shield to those who take refuge in him. **Do not add to his words**, or he will rebuke you and prove you a liar" (Proverbs 30:5).

> **"Do not go beyond what is written"** (1 Corinthians 4:6).

Think about how restrictive and liberating these commandments are! Think about how much better it would be if authors, pastors and teachers would take to heart their meaning? One thing is certain; The Word of God is sufficient and we do not need, nor should we rely on Man as we seek the Truth which is Yeshua the Messiah, called Jesus Christ.

There is so much more, but you get the idea about how Yahweh teaches me. He has also shown me many things in His Word about prophecy and I will be sharing those with you as we go through this book. However, as we have just learned, we each must go to the Word ourselves to see what God is saying. We cannot afford to be followers of Man. I am a man. Do not follow me. Follow Yahweh, the God of the Bible.

Let me show you what I have seen and heard from Yahweh about the horses and riders of Revelation's first four seals.

Revelation's Horses and Riders

The revelation I received from the Lord about the horses and riders came to me over several years starting in about 2001 as I was studying the Seals of Revelation and writing my first book, "Of the Last Days: Listen, I Tell You A Mystery."

Here is what I wrote in chapter 8 "Of the Last Days" book:

Opening of the first six seals

As the seals of the scroll are opened, John sees a sequence of events that will affect earth in the last days. As the first four seals are opened they reveal four horses and their riders. When each seal is opened the rider and horse are told to "Come!" John then describes what happens on the earth as each has its effect. There appears to be some connection between the heavenly scene of the horses and riders coming Fourth and the earthly consequences. However, based on what is written it is impossible to understand how these things are connected. The significance of these horses and riders has been debated and speculated about for centuries and it is unlikely that we can resolve this mystery in our study.

This prophecy like various others is most likely given to us so we will see the sovereign hand of God in its fulfillment, not so we can predict the future. However, as we consider these things we would be remiss if we didn't review the Scripture which appears to be related to these events.

First, as we review the scriptural record we find that the Jewish people referred to Pharaoh and his army as "the horse and its rider," as we see written in Exodus 15.

> Then Moses and the Israelites sang this song to the LORD: "I will sing to the LORD, for he is highly exalted. **The horse** and **its rider** he has hurled into the sea. The LORD is my strength and my song; he has become my salvation. He is my God, and I will praise him, my father's God, and I will exalt him. The LORD is a warrior; the LORD is his name. Pharaoh's chariots and his army he has hurled into the sea (Exodus 15:1-4).

The horse represented the people - the army of Egypt - and the rider - Pharaoh - their leader. If this analogy holds true in the Revelation vision it could mean that the horses will represent certain countries and the riders their leaders.

In the prophecies of Zechariah we also find horses of different colors described in connection with the things that are taking place on earth. Perhaps we may gain insight from these prophecies as we consider the four horses of Revelation. When Zechariah inquired regarding the horses he saw in his vision, this is what he was told.

> 'They are the ones the LORD has sent to go throughout the earth.' And they reported to the angel of the LORD, who was standing among the myrtle trees, 'We have gone throughout the earth and found the whole world at rest and in peace' (Zechariah 1:10).

There is another vision in which Zechariah describes horses of four colors. The colors of these four horses may even match the four colors of the four horses in Revelation. These horses are said to be the four spirits of heaven which go out to the four points of the earth.

> The first chariot had red horses, the second black, the third white, and the fourth dappled-- all of them powerful. I asked the angel who was speaking to me, 'What are these, my lord?' The angel answered me, 'These are the four spirits of heaven, going out from standing in the presence of the Lord of the whole world. The one with the black horses is going toward the north country, the one with the white horses toward the west, and the one with the dappled horses toward the south' (Zechariah 6:2-6).

There is still another aspect to consider as we attempt to determine the meaning of the four horses and their riders. When will they ride? As we consider this question, we can't help but notice the similarities between the first four seals and what Jesus called the beginning of the birth pains in the Olivet Discourse. In both cases Jesus is the one describing what will take place in the [time of the end and the] last days.

I also wrote about the first four seals in chapter six of my 2006 book, "The Complete Idiot's Guide to the Last Days." Here is what I wrote.

The Trouble with Heavenly Horsemen

When the first seal is opened John sees a white horse and rider. This part of what John saw is most likely a supernatural vision. No one on earth will have seen a white horse and rider when this event takes place. However, the people on earth will be able to see the corresponding natural events. This type of relationship between the supernatural and natural is described in other places in the biblical record. For example, in chapter one of Zechariah, we're told that the horses, in the supernatural realm, are supernatural beings under the direction God with assigned responsibilities in regard to events on earth. In Zechariah 6, we are also told that different colored horses are assigned certain areas of the earth. In Zechariah, the white horse goes to the west, the red horse goes to the east, the black horse goes to the north and the dappled or pale horse goes to the south. Zechariah's directions are from the location of Israel which is always the case, with the prophets of God. This information about the different colored horses will prove helpful as we consider the horses and riders of Revelation.

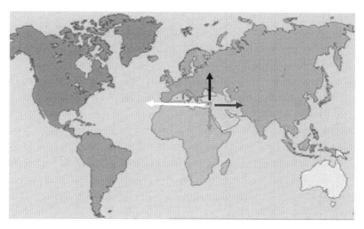

White horse: West = USA

So, we now know that when John writes about a horse and rider he is describing something God is doing in the supernatural realm which will correspond to initiate events that will happen on earth. Now, let's see what will happen as each of the seals is broken during Day 6 (of the Last Days) and the four horsemen of Revelation ride.

In the vision when the first seal is opened, a white horse and rider come out. The rider has a bow and he rode out as a conqueror determined to conquer. Since the white horse has been assigned to the west, the west will go out conquering and determined to conquer. Due west from Jerusalem crosses northern Africa and extends to the United States of America.

When the second seal is broken open, a red horse and rider come out. Its rider was given power and a large sword to take peace from the earth and to make men kill each other. Since the red horse has been assigned the east, the east will have a powerful weapon or army and will take peace from the earth which will cause men to kill each other. Due east from Jerusalem crosses Jordan, Saudi Arabia, Iraq, **Iran**, Pakistan, India and extends to China.

When the third seal is opened, a black horse comes out. Its rider held a pair of scales and a quart of wheat and three quarts of barley sold for a day's wages. Since the black horse has been assigned the north, the north will cause great damage to grain production. True north of Jerusalem crosses Lebanon, Syria, and Turkey and extends to **Russia**.

When the fourth seal is opened, a pale horse and rider come out. They were given power over a fourth of the earth to kill by sword, famine and plague, and by the wild beasts. Since the pale horse has been assigned the south, the south has power over a quarter of the earth to kill by sword, famine and plague. South of Jerusalem is Africa.

Since these earlier writings in 2001 and 2006 the Lord has given me greater revelation regarding the first four seals of Revelation. I now have a comprehensive understanding of the first seal prophecy and how it was fulfilled.

In 2009 Yahweh spoke to me in the Spirit and told me the identity of the Red Horse of Revelation's Second Seal.

With the information that God provided through the Prophets we now have sufficient information to anticipate and prepare for the Second, Third and Fourth Seals of Revelation. Here is a word the Lord has given me. It helps me to realize the extent of the information we have available through Scripture regarding the Time of the End.

When Christ was describing the End Time He said this,

> "Be on your guard. **I have told you everything ahead of time**" (Mark 13:23).

In the next few chapters we will be discussing each of the first four seals of revelation. With what we can now know, we will be able identify what has already happened and be able to anticipate what will soon be taking place on earth.

This we know:

- Revelation's Seal prophecies will span the Time of the End.
- Like birth pains, wars will increase in size and frequency.
- A horse and rider is a nation's army and its leader.
- The colored horses were assigned by God.
- Scripture tells us everything ahead of time.

Chapter 4
Rider on the White Horse

In this chapter we will be examining Revelation's First Seal horse and rider and why this prophecy is so important to God's people.

Let God do the Talking

In order to understand what Yahweh is telling us in the seal prophecies of Revelation we must let God do the talking. In Bible study circles "Let God do the talking" is called "Let Scripture interpret Scripture." When I am presented a question in Scripture, I ask God for the answer, which He provides from Scripture.

I have found in pursuing this approach that if I ask a question which is pertinent and needed then God will show me the answer in Scripture. However, if I ask a question that is irrelevant, I will either not find an answer or I will be redirected to what I need to ask. This is the approach I will be using throughout this book.

Before we discuss the First Seal white horse and rider, let me bring you up to date on the revelation that the Lord has given me about the horses and their riders. Since this is a new teaching we need to understand the foundation of this interpretation first. Then we will be able to build on it for the details of these critically important prophecies.

In the last chapter I introduced you to the first four seals of Revelation based on my earlier writings. Now, we will be discussing how I see them today.

What are the foundational parts to these prophecies that we must know in order to correctly interpret the first four seals?

Four Horses and Riders

As we read the first four seal prophecies, we notice that all four have some things in common. As each seal is opened a different colored horse comes Fourth. The first is white, the second is fiery red, the third is black and the fourth is pale. We are also told that each horse has a rider.

Therefore, if we hope to understand the meaning of these first four seal prophecies we must know the answer to these two questions:

- What do the four colored horses symbolize?
- What does a horse and rider symbolize?

First, what is symbolized by the colored horses? Do they tell us something we need to know in order to correctly understanding these prophecies? Yes, the colors symbolize something critical to a correct understanding of these prophecies.

To understand what the four different colored horses symbolize, let's search Scripture to see if God will tell us about these four horses. Is there any other place in Scripture or prophecy that mentions four colored horses?

Yes, there is only one other place in Scripture which makes reference to four different colored horses. We find them described in Zechariah's prophecies. Zechariah received many prophecies from God about the Time of the End which correspond to prophecies recorded in the book of Revelation.

In our particular example, Zechariah saw four colored horses as he recorded in chapter six. The horses in Zechariah's vision also appear to be similar or even the same as the four colored horses in Revelation chapter six. Zechariah was told about the four different colored horses. Here is what he wrote:

> "I looked up again--and there before me were four chariots coming out from between two mountains--mountains of bronze! The first chariot had red horses, the second black, the third white, and the fourth dappled--all of them powerful. I asked the angel who was speaking to me, 'What are these, my lord?' The angel answered me, **'These are the four spirits of heaven, going out from standing in the presence of the Lord of the whole world.** The one with the black horses is going toward the north country, the one with the white horses toward the west, and the one with the dappled horses toward the south" (Zechariah 6:1-8).

The four colored horses; red, black, white and dappled **are the four spirits** of heaven that go out to the whole world. The black horses go to the north, the white go toward the west and the dappled go to the south which leaves the red horses to go toward the east.

Some Bible translations state that the white horses go toward the west and some do not. Because, there is no other place in Scripture that provides a direct connection to the four colored horses of Revelation, we should at least take this information into consideration as we attempt to interpret the significance of the horses of Revelation chapter six.

There is also a slight difference between the prophet's descriptions of one of the four horses. In Revelation John describes one of the horses as pale. In Zechariah the prophet describes this horse as dappled. Could these be two seemingly different descriptions of Revelation's fourth horse actually be of the same horse? Only God knows. Never-the-less, this information may be very important and we should keep it in mind as we attempt to understand the prophecies described in the first four seals of Revelation.

Where the horses were assigned.

According to Zechariah 6, the horses **are the four spirits** of heaven that go out from the Lord. The white horses go to the west, the red horses go to the east, the black horses go to the north and the dappled go to the south.

Assigned to the West, East, North and South of where?

We should be aware that, unless otherwise stated, all biblical prophecies are written from the perspective of Jerusalem, Israel. This would mean that the four colored horses have been assigned to the west, east, north and south of Israel as geographically displayed on the map below:

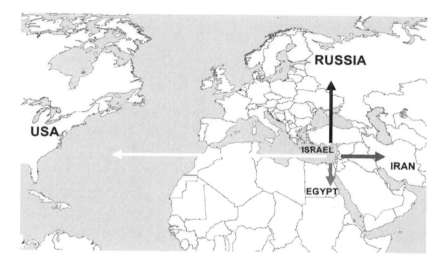

Now, we know where in the world the four colored horses were assigned by God. With this information we will know where to look as Christ opens each of the first four seals.

1. When the first seal opens, look to the West
2. When the second seal opens, look to the East.
3. When the third seal opens, look to the North.
4. When the fourth seal opens, look to the South.

Just as each of the first four seals of Revelation has a horse, each horse also has a rider. Now, we need to understand the symbolism of "horse and rider" in order to correctly interpret these first four prophecies.

What is a horse and rider? Once again we are very fortunate because Yahweh has used the terms "horse and rider" to describe both historical as well as prophetic events. Here is an example from Exodus:

> "Then Moses and the Israelites sang this song to Yahweh: I will sing to Yahweh, for he is highly exalted. **The horse and its rider** he has hurled into the sea. ... **Pharaoh**'s chariots **and his army** he has hurled into the sea" (Exodus 15:1-4).

In the Exodus story, Pharaoh is the rider and his army is the horse.

These next two prophecies further illustrate how God uses "horse and rider" to symbolize nation's armies and their leaders.

> "You are my war club, my weapon for battle-- with you I shatter nations, with you I destroy kingdoms, with you **I shatter horse and rider**, with you I shatter chariot and driver" (Jeremiah 51:20-21).

> "On that day I will strike **every horse with panic and its rider with madness**," declares the LORD. "I will keep a watchful eye over the house of Judah, but I will blind all the horses of the nations" (Zechariah 12:4).

These descriptions of "horse and rider" in prophecy clearly indicate that God uses "horse and rider" to represent a nation's "army and its leader."

Therefore, as we examine the horses and riders of Revelation's first four seals we can now understand what they symbolize.

- Horse = A nations Military
- Rider = A nations Leader

As each seal is opened, a national leader and his army will begin to fulfill the prophecy described in Revelation chapter six. Therefore, as each seal is opened another leader and his army will start another war in the Time of the End.

First Seal Prophecy

Here is how the first seal prophecy is described in Revelation:

> "I watched as the Lamb opened the first of the seven seals. Then I heard one of the four living creatures say in a voice like thunder, 'Come!' I looked, and there before me was a white horse! Its rider held a bow, and he was given a crown, and he rode out as a conqueror bent on conquest" (Revelation 6:1-2).

Rider on the White Horse

When Christ opened the first of the seven seals, we are told that the white horse has a rider. The rider on the white horse was a leader from the West.

What Man Thinks

Before we continue, let's look at a common mistake that has been made when trying to identify the rider on the white horse. This error in interpretation was made many years ago. Unfortunately, it is still being repeated today by many teachers who rely on the teachings of Man over and above the Word of God.

In the book of Revelation we find that there are two riders on white horses. The first rider is one we have seen in Revelation's First Seal prophecy. The second rider is seen in Revelation chapter 19. Below is the description of the second horse and rider:

"I saw heaven standing open and there before me was a white horse, whose rider is called Faithful and True. With justice he judges and makes war. His eyes are like blazing fire, and on his head are many crowns. He has a name written on him that no one knows but he himself. He is dressed in a robe dipped in blood, and **his name is the Word of God**" (Revelation 19:11-13).

This second rider is Christ, the Word of God.

Because the second rider is clearly Christ, many people have assumed that the first rider on the white horse must either be Christ or he must be a false Christ. That is why many people still think the first rider on the white horse is Antichrist.

These people appear to be using Scripture to make their interpretation. However, they are taking the prophecy out of context and jumping to conclusions. The first seal prophecy is not just about a white horse and its rider. In its context this prophecy is about four colored horses and their riders. Therefore, we must look at all four horses and riders to get the picture in context, not just one horse and rider but all four.

Mistaking the first horse and rider for Christ or the Antichrist leads people into other very serious mistakes.

Many that interpret this first rider as Christ tend to believe the prophecy started about 2,000 years ago with Christ. These people are often called "Preterists" because they see Revelation's prophecies as historical, thinking that they were written about Rome's persecution of the Church.

Those that believe that the first rider on the white horse is the Antichrist, also assume that the seven seals span the last seven years when the Antichrist appears and rules the earth. These people are often called "Dispensationalists" or "Pre-Tribulationists" because they believe that the "Rapture" of the Church will occur before the last seven years when the Antichrist will be in power.

However, both of these old teachings of Man are inconsistent with what Yahweh says will happen.

What God Says

As we will see from Scripture, the seals will span a much longer period of time than just seven years. The seals will span the entire Time of the End which Christ said would last less than a generation. Therefore, as we will see the First Seal will start the Time of the End and the Seventh Seal will close the Time of the End.

Therefore, based on this new interpretation from Scripture, the white horse and rider represented an army and its leader from the West.

We are also told in the first seal prophecy that the "rider held a bow." It appears from Scripture that this bow has two symbolic meanings.

First, a bow is a military weapon and has military symbolism. ① However, in our prophecy, that symbolism is redundant because we already know that the riders of the horses are leaders of their armies. Since we already know that, it is more likely that God is telling us something else that will help us.

The second symbolic meaning seems to indicate that this bow is ② God's bow and is connected with the beginning of Time of the End. This would mean that the bow has spiritual significance in a similar way as the colored horses are four spirits of heaven.

Below is an End Time prophecy from Habakkuk that gives that impression. See what you think:

> "Were you angry with the rivers, O Yahweh? Was your wrath against the streams? Did you rage against the sea when you rode with your horses and your victorious chariots? **You uncovered your bow**, you called for many arrows" (Habakkuk 3:8-9).

Therefore, when the first seal was opened, the rider on the white horse was the commander-in-chief of the military from the west and had something to do with **Yahweh uncovering His bow**. I interpret this as symbolizing the starting point of the Time of the End. If so, this rider holding a bow would tend to support the idea that the first seal starts something regarding Yahweh End Time plan.

What historically happened after the first seal was opened?

He was given a Crown

Then the rider on the white horse was given a crown. The Greek word for crown in this verse indicates that it is a victor's crown.

From this we can determine that sometime after the first seal was opened the leader from the west won a victory, "he was given a crown".

What else happened after the seal was opened?

He Rode Out as a Conqueror

After the first seal was opened, the leader from the west "rode out as a conqueror bent on conquest". He left his country in the west and went out to another country as a conqueror. But that's not all.

He was Bent on Conquest

Not only did he go out as a conqueror, but we he was also bent on conquest. In other words, he was determined to conquer in war.

Now that we have reviewed this first Seal Prophecy from Revelation, let's see how this prophecy was historically fulfilled.

First Seal Prophecy Fulfilled

The white horse was assigned to the west of Israel. Due west from Israel, as we can see from the map below, is the United States of America.

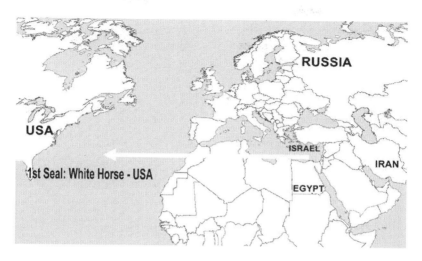

Therefore, the events of this prophecy relate to the United States of America and its leader at the time the First Seal is opened.

When was the first seal opened?

Rider in the White House

9/11

On September 11, 2001, Christ opened the first seal of Revelation. When He opened the first seal the rider on the white horse was holding a bow. On 9/11/2001 the President of the United States was the Commander-in-Chief of the U.S. Military and he was about to start a war that would initiate or instigate End Time events.

After the First Seal was opened on 9/11, "he was given a crown". In 2004, George W. Bush won an election and a second term as President of the United States and Commander-in-Chief of the U.S. Military. Therefore, after 9/11 he was received a victor's crown.

What else happen after 9/11?

Rode out as a Conqueror

Also after the first seal opened on 9/11, the Commander-in-Chief "rode out as a conqueror." In 2001, under his leadership the U.S. Military went to Afghanistan and drove the Taliban out of that country.

Then again, after 9/11, the Commander-in-Chief "rode out as a conqueror." In 2003 the U.S. Military attacked and conquered Iraq and Saddam Hussein, the President of Iraq.

Determined to Win the War on Terror

In addition, during his two terms as President U.S.A. and Commander-in-Chief of the U.S. Military – the rider on the white horse - remained "bent on conquest". He was determined to win the "War on Terror" which he had declared.

These recent historical events precisely and accurately fulfilled each detail of the first seal prophecy of the Book of Revelation. Let's review the prophecy one more time so we have this clearly in mind:

> "I looked, and there before me was a white horse! Its rider held a bow, and he was given a crown, and he rode out as a conqueror bent on conquest" (Revelation 6:2).

The first seal of Revelation is the first of three major prophecies which identify and confirm that the Time of the End has come.

There is another prophecy which also seems to point to the 9/11 event, when the first seal of Revelation was opened. This Old Testament prophecy appears to reference the collapse of the Twin Towers in New York City on 9/11/2001. Here is how that prophecy reads:

> "Take up your positions around Babylon, all you who draw the bow. Shoot at her! Spare no arrows, for she has sinned against the LORD. Shout against her on every side!… **her towers fall**" (Jeremiah 50:14-15).

We also find an aspect of this in Zechariah chapter six which may add further support to this interpretation.

Let's take a close look at Zechariah's prophecy again.

> "I looked up again--and there before me were four chariots **coming out from between two mountains--mountains of bronze**! The first chariot had red horses, the second black, the third white, and the fourth dappled--all of them powerful. I asked the angel who was speaking to me, 'What are these, my lord?' The angel answered me, 'These are the four spirits of heaven, going out from standing in the presence of the Lord of the whole world. The one with the black horses is going toward the north country, the one with the white horses toward the west, and the one with the dappled horses toward the south" (Zechariah 6:1-8).

If we note that "bronze" is a man-made metal, then we could understand this verse to say something like this,

> "I looked up again--and there before me were four chariots **coming out from between two man made mountains**"

or even,

> **I looked up again—and there before me were four chariots coming out from between the twin towers of the World Trade Center.**

From what we read in Scripture and the historical events since 9/11, the fulfillment of the first seal prophecy appears to serve as a prophetic witness to the Time of the End. This is the first witness to the Time of the End. Below is how this would appear on a timeline.

Time of the End: 1ˢᵗ Seal

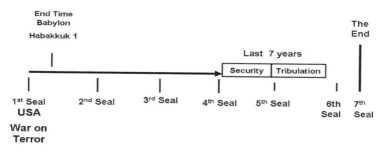

Before we examine the 2ⁿᵈ Seal which is the next Time of the End prophecy to be fulfilled, I would like to point out something we should know about the First Seal prophecy. The prophet Habakkuk also wrote about some of the events that would take place after the First Seal was opened. Compare Habakkuk's first chapter account to the history of what happened when the US Military went out conquering following 9/11.

Don't forget Habakkuk.

Here is some of what Habakkuk wrote about that.

> "**I am raising up the Babylonians**, that ruthless and impetuous people, **who sweep across the whole earth** to seize dwelling places not their own. They are a feared and dreaded people; **they are a law to themselves** and promote their own honor. Their horses are swifter than leopards, fiercer than wolves at dusk. Their cavalry gallops headlong; **their horsemen come from afar. They fly like a vulture swooping to devour**; they all come bent on violence. **Their hordes advance like a desert wind** and gather prisoners like sand. They deride kings and scoff at rulers. They laugh at all fortified cities; they build earthen ramps and capture them. Then they sweep past like the wind and go on-- guilty men, whose own strength is their god" (Habakkuk 1:6-11).

I should point out that Habakkuk's prophecies are specifically stated by God to be about the Babylonians in the appointed Time of the End.

Before we move on, let me share with you something I saw that I believe offers even more support to the idea that 9/11 marked the opening of the First Seal. It's a Youtube.com video titled, **"ASTOUNDING REVELATION - GOD'S JUDGMENT ON AMERICA – REVEALED"**[1] It provides some good Scriptural support.

Missed Wake Up Call.

Now, the First Seal prophecy was God's first wake up call for His Church. If the Church had been awake as Christ commanded they would have been able to recognize that the First Seal Prophecy had been fulfilled. However, the Church was not awake and they did not recognize from Scripture what had happened.

Not only was the Church asleep but they also failed to wake up. When the First Seal opened on 9/11 many of the churches initially appeared to be waking up as they began to seek God in prayer. This continued for several months. It was as though the churches were trying to awaken. However, they did not wake up and within a year following 9/11 all the churches had returned to their deep sleep, doing just what they had been doing before the First Seal opened.

Christ wanted His Church to be awake. When Christ was telling His followers about the Time of the End in what we call the Olivet Discourse, He warned them to stay awake, be alert and keep watch. The passage below from Mark's gospel captures Christ's warning,

---

[1]http://www.youtube.com/watch?v=JW6roFN7NAE&list=FLXNJGzvnMfDY9yUUmjL vQWA&index=1&feature=plpp_video

> "**Be on guard! Be alert! You do not know when that time will come**. ... Therefore **keep watch** because you do not know when the owner of the house will come back ... If he comes suddenly, **do not let him find you sleeping.** What I say to you, I say to everyone: **'Watch!'**" (Mark 13:33-37)

Christ wanted His Church to stay awake. He also knew that they would not be awake when the Time of the End began. Therefore, He planned to wake them when Revelation's Second Seal prophecy is fulfilled.

Every follower of Christ has a personal responsibility to obey Christ's instructions to be on guard, be alert, stay awake and keep watch.

However, to those who have been given leadership responsibility in the household of God, they will be held to a higher accountability. In Matthew 24:45-51, Christ warned those He left in charge that He would come and cut them to pieces if they did not provide their food (Word) at the proper time (Time of the End).

> "Who then is the faithful and wise servant, whom the master has put **in charge of the servants in his household** to give them their food at the proper time? ... But suppose **that servant is wicked** and says to himself, **'My master is staying away a long time**' (Matthew 24:45-48).

The assigned watchmen who were the pastors, priests and shepherds in God's household did not provide the Word at the proper time. Therefore, the Household of God remained asleep for over ten years after the Time of the End had already begun in 2001.

Yahweh prophesied about the Time of the End shepherds in the prophets. Below is what Yahweh said through Isaiah:

"**Israel's watchmen are blind**, they all lack knowledge; they are all mute dogs, they cannot bark; they lie around and dream, they love to sleep. They are dogs with mighty appetites; they never have enough. **They are shepherds who lack understanding**; they all turn to their own way, each seeks his own gain" (Isaiah 56:10-11).

God also explained that the churches would be asleep when the Time of the End began. Some of this will certainly be as a result of the pastor's blindness and lack of understanding. Christ explained this in the parable of the Ten Virgins. At the Time of the End all the churches would be asleep. Here is how he described this End Time situation in Matthew 25:

"At that time the kingdom of heaven will be like ten virgins [church] who took their lamps and went out to meet the bridegroom. ... The bridegroom was a long time in coming, and **they all became drowsy and fell asleep**. At midnight **the cry rang out**: 'Here comes the bridegroom! Come out to meet him!' Then **all the virgins woke up** and trimmed their lamps" (Matthew 24:1-7).

Notice in this parable that Christ indicated that at first all those who are waiting for Christ would be asleep - all of them. Then a great cry rang out and all of them woke up. It will be just like this when the Second Seal of Revelation is opened. A great cry will ring out and all the churches will wake up to the realization the Time of the End Has Come and the End of the Age is near.

Note: That great wake up cry that wakes up all the churches is recorded in Jeremiah 51:54.

Now let's examine the Second Seal witness to the Time of the End and find out what it is that is going to wake up the sleeping churches.

What we now know:

- Horses symbolize armies and their riders their leaders.
- Where God has assigned the four horses of Revelation.
- That the First Seal war prophecy has been fulfilled.
- That the churches are still asleep, but not for long.

Chapter 5
Rider on the Red Horse

In this chapter we will be examining Revelation's Second Seal Horse and Rider and discussing why this prophecy is very important to God's people.

After the First Seal was opened, George W. Bush and the U.S. Military fulfilled the First Seal prophecy when they went out conquering in the War on Terror. In 2001 the U.S. went to Afghanistan conquering the Taliban. In 2003 the U.S. went to Iraq conquering Saddam Hussein.

When Christ opens the second seal the rider on the red horse will start world war. It will be the Second Seal crisis which finally awakens all the churches to the fact that the Time of the End has come. Here is how the second seal prophecy is described in most English Bibles:

> "When the Lamb opened the second seal, I heard the second living creature say, "Come!" Then another horse came out, a fiery red one. **Its rider was given power to take peace from the earth** and to make men slay each other. **To him was given a large sword**" (Revelation 6:3-4).

As we previously read in Zechariah 6, the red horse is one of the four spirits of heaven that has gone out from the presence of the Lord. Zechariah's prophecy indicates that the white horses were assigned to the West and the red horses to the East of Israel.

Rider on the Red Horse

Now that the First Seal has been opened and fulfilled we know that the Second Seal prophecy is the next seal prophecy to be opened and fulfilled. A leader and his military from the East of Israel will start World War.

Let's take another look at our world map. The map indicates where the colored horses of prophecy have been assigned by God, based on Zechariah chapter six.

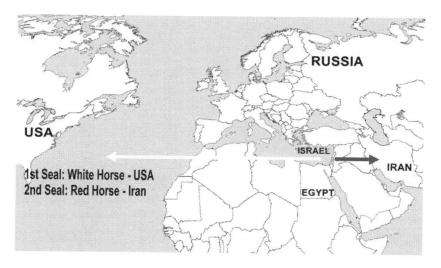

We are told that the second seal military leader will be "given power to take peace from the earth and to make men slay each other." Therefore, the opening of the second seal will mark the beginning of world war.

When the second seal opens, war on earth will have reached a new level, going from regional conflicts to global. The major world powers like Russia, China, the United States and others will begin to openly oppose each other in a global struggle.

The second seal will mark the beginning of global conflict in the Time of the End. It does not mark the end itself. This Second Seal war will last for years before the Third Seal battle begins. Bible prophecy is also clear that nuclear weapons will be used at the beginning of the Second Seal war and will be used again in larger scale in the Third Seal battle.

The Second Seal war will likely be called World War Three. The Third Seal war would likely be an extension of World War III.

How will World War III begin, at the opening of the Second Seal?

World War III

In the Second Seal prophecy, after we were told that peace is taken from the earth we were told that the rider on the red horse would be given a large sword. Let's examine exactly what this prophecy says:

> "To him was given a large [megas] sword [machaira]." (Revelation" 6:4).

This part of the prophecy seems to indicate something about how the leader from the east of Israel will take peace from the earth.

Because most militaries today do not use large swords, let's examine the original Greek words which are translated as "large sword". Understanding the meaning of these Greek words will help us determine what the prophecy means in the context of modern warfare.

The Greek words for "large sword" are 'megas' and 'machaira'.

'Megas' means; large, great, loud or mighty.

'Machaira' means; sword and it comes from the root word 'mache' meaning battle, controversy or fighting.

In today's military context the second seal prophecy seems to indicate that the rider on the red horse was given either "**a great battle**" or that he was given "**a mighty weapon**."

Now, we have a couple of ideas of how peace will be taken from the earth; either a large weapon (nuclear weapon) or great victory in a large battle.

Second Seal Prophecy Fulfilled

Before we consider the rider on the red horse, let me point out that this second seal prophecy is the second major Time of the End prophecy to be fulfilled.

This second major End Time biblical prophecy also will serve as a second witness to the Time of the End.

> "Every matter must be established by the testimony of two or three witnesses" (2 Corinthians 13:1).

When the second seal prophecy is finally fulfilled we will have our second witness to the End Time. Then we will be able to scripturally establish that - the Time Has Come.

It is the year 2012 and ten years have passed since the first seal of Revelation was opened on 9/11. Based on what Christ said about the Time of the End being less than a generation, we must be very close to when the Second Seal will be opened. If so, it seems likely that we could have a good idea of who the Second Seal red horse and rider will be?

There are two answers to this question.

First, from a worldly perspective; who seems to be the most logical candidate to be the Red Horse of Revelation?

Second, from a biblical perspective; who does Yahweh say the Red Horse will be?

Let's take a brief look at the worldly perspective.

Who may Fulfill the Second Seal Prophecy

Iran seems like a logical candidate!

Background Iran:[2]

For decades the Islamic Republic of Iran has been increasingly developing its own military industrial complex. Today, Iran produces tanks, armored personnel carriers, submarines, naval ships, fighter planes, unmanned aerial vehicles, advanced guided and ballistic missiles. Following the overthrow of the Shah of Iran and the American Hostage Crisis of 1979, Iran has been operating under numerous military embargos imposed by the West.[3]

During this same period Iran's, anti-U.S. and anti-Israel, ruling Islamic Shia party has become politically more aggressive in exerting its influence regionally. Under the supreme leader, **Ayatollah Ali Khamenei** and its President **Mahmoud Ahmadinejad**, Iran has called for the elimination of Israel and the removal of the United States of America from the Middle East region.

More recently, as Iran relentlessly develops its nuclear capabilities, sanctions from the United States and the United Nations have intensified. The West wants to stop Iran from obtaining nuclear weapons and altering the balance of power in the Middle East and the world.

Current Crisis:

---

[2] http://en.wikipedia.org/wiki/Iran

[3] http://en.wikipedia.org/wiki/Sanctions_against_Iran

A decade of unsuccessful United Nations sanctions seems to have only increased Iran's resolve to achieve its nuclear goals. In the final months of the Bush administration, and in spite of numerous incentives from the European Union, Iran has redoubled its efforts to reach it nuclear goal.

Because all negotiations, sanctions and incentives have failed to stop Iran, there appear to be only two options remaining; attack Iran nuclear sites or impose a naval blockade to force Iran to stop its nuclear program.

Because the Bible does not seem to mention an attack on Iran during the Time of the End, a naval blockade appears to be the most likely option that the West will take. With the incredible military might of the U.S. Aircraft-Carrier Strike Groups, this option seems like it would be effective in forcing Iran to the table.

However, there are several things to consider in regard to this course of action.

First, to impose a naval blockade on Iran would put the U.S. Navy in harms way. To blockade Iran would require that a considerable military force be placed just off the shores of Iran; in the Persian Gulf, the Strait of Hormuz and the Gulf of Oman.

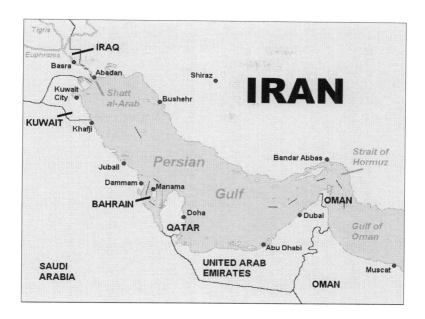

Second, Iran is reported to have several advanced weapons systems for fighting naval battles, including: submarines, rocket propelled torpedo with a 230 mph velocity, anti-ship guided missiles with a velocity of twice the speed of sound, and ship-to-ship guided missiles with a range of over 200 kilometers.

Third, Iran is not known to back down under pressure. Therefore, Iran seems to be a very logical candidate to be the Red Horse of Revelation's Second Seal. The world can try to guess who will start World War III, but Yahweh already knows and here is what He said,

> "Be on your guard. I have told you everything ahead of time" (Mark 13:23).

If God has told us everything, then He must have already told us who the Red Horse will be.

He has, the Red Horse symbolizes IRAN!

IRAN will Fulfill the Second Seal Prophecy

How do I know that Iran is the country that will be taking peace from the earth? There are three reasons why I believe this was given to me by Yahweh, the God of the Bible.

First, I have already explained how I was led by God to understand some of the symbolism of Revelation's first four seals.

That the "horses and riders" symbolize "armies and their leaders" and that the "four colored horses" symbolize the countries which will start each of the first four seal wars, like the U.S. started the War on Terror.

Second, in September of 2009, the Lord spoke to me in the spirit and said, "The red horse symbolizes Iran. I have stirred up the kings of the Medes because my purpose is to destroy Babylon."

The Lord's statement to me both told me and showed me a key piece of the Second Seal Prophecy. The first sentence of what He said, "The red horse symbolizes Iran." identified to me, who the Second Seal country would be.

Third, the second sentence of what He said I later identified as something that Yahweh had given to Jeremiah regarding the End Time Babylonians. Here is what Yahweh told Jeremiah about the Time of the End:

> "Sharpen the arrows, take up the shields! **Yahweh has stirred up the kings of the Medes, because his purpose is to destroy Babylon**. Yahweh will take vengeance, vengeance for his temple. Lift up a banner against the walls of Babylon! Reinforce the guard, station the watchmen, **prepare an ambush**! Yahweh will carry out his purpose, his decree against the people of Babylon. You who live by many waters and are rich in treasures, your end has come, the time for you to be cut off' (Jeremiah 51:11-13).

Here is what this passage means to me and why it confirms to me that Iran is the Red Horse of Revelation. A) The ancient Medes would be the present day Iranians. B) I know from Revelation chapter 17 and Daniel 8 and 11 that it will be the Antichrist who gets credit for destroying End Time Babylon. Since, the Antichrist does not come from Iran this prophecy must be describing something that Iran does that leads to Babylon's destruction, not the destruction itself. C) The word that Yahweh gave me regarding Iran fits like a missing peace of the puzzle in a large prophetic picture that God has provided regarding the Time of the End.

I realize this brief explanation may not explain all the details of how this confirms that Iran is the Red Horse of Revelation's Second Seal. However, I will be filling in all the pieces to the prophetic puzzle as we proceed through this book.

Before we move on, I will update our timeline with the 2nd Seal. The 2nd Seal timeline connects End Time Babylon and Habakkuk 2 to the time of the 2nd Seal. We will be discussing this connection in chapter 6 titled End Time Babylon.

Time of the End: 2nd Seal

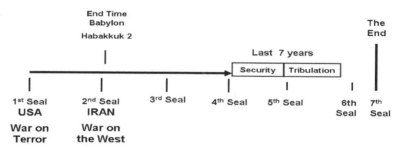

Now, let's review another aspect of the Second Seal prophecy.

After the two witnesses speak.

When we have seen the fulfillment of the first two seal prophecies of Revelation we will have heard from two scriptural witnesses confirming that the Time of the End has come. The Bible says it takes two or three witnesses to establish a matter.

Will there be a third witness, so we can be absolutely certain? After all, confirming the Time of the End is extremely important to God's people. Would He leave us with just two witnesses?

No! Because being certain about where we are in the Time of the End is critically important, Yahweh has indeed provided a third Witness to the End Time. We will be discussing that third witness in chapter 6, End Time Babylonians.

Only Yahweh knows exactly what will happen and when. However, He has given these prophecies to us, His people, so that we can understand and know what to do. That is why He has provided these prophecies ahead of time so His people can be alert, on guard and keeping watch.

As we already know, before the Second Seal opened God's people were all asleep. However, once they all awake to the realization that the Time of the End has come, many things will change.

Let's discuss one of those changes before we move on and consider the third witness and its impact on Yahweh's people.

When all the churches wake up.

We should also be aware that it was Christ who strongly warned His Church not to sleep. Here is what He said,

> "Be on guard! Be alert! You do not know when that time will come…. Therefore keep watch … If he comes suddenly, **do not let him find you sleeping.** What I say to you, I say to everyone: 'Watch!'" (Mark 13:33-37)

Let's look at a couple of His warnings in Revelation,

"Remember, therefore, what you have received and heard; obey it, and repent. But **if you do not wake up**, I will come like a thief, and you will not know at what time I will come to you" (Revelation 3:3).

"Behold, I come like a thief! **Blessed is he who stays awake**" (Revelation 16:15).

We can clearly see that Christ wanted His Church to be awake! However, He also knew that they would fall asleep as we have read in the "parable of the Ten Virgins" in Matthew 25:1-7.

He also specifically warned the pastors that there would be dire consequences if they failed to follow His instructions. Here is an excerpt from that warning,

> "If the owner of the house had known at what time of night the thief was coming, he would have kept watch and would not have let his house be broken into. ... Who then is the faithful and wise servant, **whom the master has put in charge of the servants in his household** to give them their food at the proper time? ... But suppose that servant is wicked and says to himself, 'My master is staying away a long time,' ... The master of that servant will come on a day when he does not expect him and ... cut him to pieces and assign him a place with the hypocrites, where there will be weeping and gnashing of teeth" (Matthew 24:43-51).

God also foretold that the shepherds would be caught off guard by the coming Time of the End. For example:

> "Israel's watchmen are blind, **they all lack knowledge**; they are all mute dogs, they cannot bark; they lie around and dream, they love to sleep. ... They are **shepherds who lack understanding; they all turn to their own way,** each seeks his own gain" (Isaiah 56:10-11).

Yahweh is not pleased with the shepherds who where in charge when the Time had come. Here is what He said through Ezekiel,

"This is what the Sovereign Yahweh says: I am against the shepherds and will hold them accountable for my flock. I will remove them from tending the flock so that the shepherds can no longer feed themselves. I will rescue my flock from their mouths, and it will no longer be food for them. ... I myself will search for my sheep and look after them" (Ezekiel 34:10-11).

There will be consequences for the shepherds as well as the flock for not staying wake and being alert to the Time of the End. All God's people should have been in their Bibles, reading about the Second Coming and keeping watch. If they had remained awake they would have been able to identify Revelation's First Seal prophecy years earlier.

Never the less, God knew this would happen. That is why He planned that they would all wake up at the Second Seal. At the Second Seal **there is still time** for the Church! **But, no time to lose!**

About those left in charge of the household of God; the pastors, shepherds, elders, teachers – heed God's Word.

"Do not take revenge, my friends, but leave room for God's wrath, for it is written: 'It is mine to avenge; I will repay,' says the Lord." (Romans 12:19).

Now that we have covered the basics regarding the Second Seal prophecy we will discuss in chapter six what Yahweh has provided as our third witness to the Time of the End. After that we will examine the Third Seal horse and rider and related prophecies in chapter seven.

What we now know:

- The Second Seal red horse symbolizes Iran.
- The rider on the red horse is Iran's President **Mahmoud Ahmadinejad**.

- When the Second Seal opens all the churches will awake.
- Church leaders will be hard pressed to explain what is happening.

Chapter 6
End Time Babylonians

In this chapter we will be examining the prophecies of Habakkuk and Jeremiah that deal with the Time of the End Babylonians and discussing why these prophecies are so important to God's people.

When the Second Seal prophecy is fulfilled it will trigger the fulfillment of several other biblical prophecies in quick succession. The fulfillment of these prophecies will establish that the Time of the End has come and at the same time help Yahweh's people identify the End Time Babylonians.

Habakkuk: End Time Prophet

Before we jump into Habakkuk's prophecies, let me introduce you to this little know Time of the End prophet. I say little known prophet because Habakkuk is rarely considered in Time of the End discussions. While the book of Revelation is almost always featured, Habakkuk gets little notice. However, that is all about to change.

When the Second Seal of Revelation is opened, all Bible churches will begin to awake and search the Scriptures regarding the Time of the End, something they should have done when the First Seal opened. When they examine Habakkuk as we are about to do, they will find some amazing prophecies which Yahweh has kept in reserve for His people, so they would be able to see who the End Time Babylonians are.

Before we dig in to Habakkuk, I want to point out two over riding statements that Yahweh made in Habakkuk. Understanding these two statements will help us open Habakkuk's prophecies so that we may see how Habakkuk becomes the third biblical witness to the Time of the End.

Habakkuk's First Overriding Statement

As I have mentioned, Habakkuk has been a grossly overlooked End Time prophet. Let's consider a couple of facts about Habakkuk before I tell you about the two statements. It seems almost everyone attributes the prophecies in Revelation to the Time of the End, as they should. This is so even though the End Time is never specifically mentioned in the book of Revelation. Also, virtually every Bible student knows that the prophecies of Daniel are Key to understanding the Time of the End. Unlike Revelation which never mentions the Time of the End, we are told in one of Daniel's prophecies that the prophecy concerns the appointed Time of the End. Here is what Yahweh said to Daniel.

> "He said: "I am going to tell you what will happen later in the time of wrath, because **the vision concerns the appointed time of the end**" (Daniel 8:19).

Now, here is where Habakkuk stands out in the field of End Time prophets. Habakkuk is the only prophet in which Yahweh made this specific statement about the appointed Time of the End. Here is what God said to Habakkuk,

"Then Yahweh replied: 'Write down the revelation and make it plain on tablets so that a herald may run with it. **For the revelation awaits an appointed time; it speaks of the end** and will not prove false. Though it linger, wait for it; it will certainly come and will not delay" (Habakkuk 2:1-3).

Yahweh told Habakkuk that this revelation speaks of the Time of the End.

Habakkuk's Second Overriding Statement

Habakkuk's second overriding statement identifies that Habakkuk's prophecies are primarily about the End Time Babylonians.

Now that the Time of the End has come, we can begin to understand the meaning of Habakkuk's long overlooked significance. The fact that Habakkuk's prophecies have not been understood until now makes perfect sense in light of Yahweh's statement to Daniel. Yahweh said,

> "Go your way, Daniel, because **the words are closed** up and sealed **until the time of the end**" (Daniel 12:9).

Now, that Yahweh's prophetic words are being opened and unsealed, let's take a look at Habakkuk's revelation to see what our third witness to the Time of the End has for us about the End Time Babylonians. In Habakkuk, Yahweh says,

> **"I am raising up the Babylonians**, that ruthless and impetuous people, who sweep across the whole earth to seize dwelling places not their own. They are a feared and dreaded people; they are a law to themselves and promote their own honor" (Habakkuk 1:6-7).

With Habakkuk's two prophetic declarations we can see that Habakkuk's prophecies deal with the End Time Babylonians.

Knowing that, we should have little difficultly identifying the Babylonians now that the Time of the End has come.

Let's consult our third witness to see what Yahweh has for us.

Habakkuk our Third Witness

Once the second seal of Revelation has been opened Habakkuk's prophecies will become easily recognizable and their significance apparent to those who read and study their Bibles.

The prophecies of Habakkuk are divided into three chapters. We will first examine chapter one which I believe has a relationship with the First Seal prophecy of Revelation. Then we will examine chapter two which will provide us with specific prophetic confirmation that the United States of America is the nation that Yahweh calls the Babylonians.

Habakkuk Chapter One

In chapter one, we are given descriptions about the Babylonians that describes the U.S.A. following 9/11 when it went to war against Iraq. After 9/11 the U.S. attacked Iraq in what was called "Iraqi Freedom." This 2003 war was part of the "War on Terror" which was declared by George W. Bush. Below is how Yahweh described to the prophet Habakkuk what the United States was going to do in 2003 when it attacked Iraq.

"Look at the nations and watch-- and be utterly amazed. For I am going to do something in your days that you would not believe, even if you were told. **I am raising up the Babylonians**, that ruthless and impetuous people, **who sweep across the whole earth** to seize dwelling places not their own. They are a feared and dreaded people; **they are a law to themselves** and promote their own honor. Their horses are swifter than leopards, fiercer than wolves at dusk. Their cavalry gallops headlong; their horsemen come from afar. **They fly like a vulture swooping to devour**; they all come bent on violence. **Their hordes advance like a desert wind** and gather prisoners like sand. **They deride kings and scoff at rulers**. They laugh at all fortified cities; they build earthen ramps and capture them. Then they sweep past like the wind and go on-- guilty men, whose own strength is their god" (Habakkuk 1:5-11).

Also in Habakkuk chapter one, Yahweh described the how the United States would be living off the bounty of its economy.

"The wicked foe pulls all of them up with hooks, he catches them in his net, **he gathers them up in his dragnet**; and so he rejoices and is glad. Therefore he sacrifices to his net and burns incense to his dragnet, for **by his net he lives in luxury and enjoys the choicest food**. Is he to keep on emptying his net, destroying nations without mercy?" (Habakkuk 1:15-17).

Habakkuk Chapter Two

In Habakkuk chapter two Yahweh's prophecies become even more detailed about what the Babylonians will do. Yahweh describes the leader of the United States, providing personal characteristics that will distinguish him from all others. Yahweh says this leader will be very popular before he becomes responsible for incredible destruction and lose of life. After that, however, everyone will be so angry with the president that they will "**taunt him with ridicule and scorn**." Here is how that is written:

"See, he is puffed up; his desires are not upright ... indeed, wine betrays him; he is arrogant and never at rest. Because he is as greedy as the grave and like death is never satisfied, he gathers to himself all the nations and takes captive all the peoples. Will not **all of them taunt him with ridicule and scorn**" (Habakkuk 2:4-6)

This description seems to describe the current U.S. President, Barack Obama. However, there are many people who may think this could describe any number of political leaders. Therefore, Yahweh has included something in His description that will help us to confirm if this is Barack Hussein Obama or not.

When the Babylonian President fulfills these prophecies as recorded in Habakkuk, one statement will help confirm who this is. That statement is this, "indeed wine betrays him."

How this statement will be fulfilled, only Yahweh knows. However, Yahweh's people will soon know just what "wine betrays him" means.

Recalling that President Obama received the "Noble Peace Prize" and reading in Habakkuk about the death and destruction this leader causes, we can imagine how all the people may taunt him.

Also in Habakkuk's prophecy Yahweh explains what will happen to the U.S. economy as a result of the president's actions.

"Will not **your creditors** suddenly arise? **Will** they not wake up and **make you tremble? Then you will become their victim.**" (Habakkuk 2:7)

Yahweh also tells us what the president does which causes this financial disaster for the Babylonians.

"**Because you** have plundered many nations, the peoples who are left will plunder you. **For you** have shed man's blood; you have destroyed lands and cities and everyone in them" (Habakkuk 2:8).

Yahweh further explains this change in fortune, here:

> **"You will be filled with shame instead of glory**. Now it is your turn! Drink and be exposed! The cup from the Lord's right hand is coming around to you, and disgrace will cover your glory. **The violence you have done <u>to Lebanon</u> will overwhelm you, and your destruction of animals will terrify you. For you have shed man's blood; you have destroyed lands and cities and everyone in them"** (Habakkuk 2:16-17).

Somehow the U.S. President will cause death and destruction in Lebanon.

Only Yahweh knows the beginning from the end and Habakkuk's prophecies about the End Time Babylonians is a good example of His power and His character. Habakkuk's prophecies are very convincing proof that Yahweh means what He says. Remember the word's of Christ when He was telling His disciples about the Time of the End and said,

> "Be on your guard. **I have told you everything ahead of time"** (Mark 13:23).

God means what He says. Yahweh says, "I have told you everything ahead of time" and Habakkuk is a good example of that.

Keep in mind that all of God's Word is written for His people. Yahweh knows how to speak with His people and His people can read and understand what He says. The rest of the world, those without the Spirit of Yahweh, cannot understand nor do they believe what Yahweh says.

Yahweh has given these prophecies to His people so that they will know what is happening. Our three prophetic witnesses will also help us to determine about how much time remains in the Time of the End and what will be happening next. That is why Christ wanted us to know about these prophecies and why He told His people to stay awake, to be alert and to keep watch!

Jeremiah has something to say.

Habakkuk was not the only prophet to write about the End Time Babylonians. Several of God's prophets wrote about the Time of the End Babylonians. The apostle John wrote about "Mystery Babylon" and "Babylon the Great" in the book of Revelation. In Revelation chapters 17 and 18 it is easy to see that Babylon the Great is a powerful nation that will exist for a short while during the Time of the End. What most people do not realize is that Yahweh told us a great deal about the End Time Babylonians hundreds of years before Revelation was written.

For example the prophet Jeremiah wrote about the Babylonians regarding the Second Seal war that we discussed in the last chapter. In Jeremiah 51, the prophet indicated that the Iranian leaders would ambush the End Time Babylonians a.k.a. the Americans. Yahweh told Jeremiah that there was going to be war, He said, "Sharpen the arrows, take up the shields!" Yahweh said that He had "stirred up the kings of the Medes." The ancient Medes are the Iranians of today. Then Yahweh indicated that there would be an "ambush" on the Babylonians because He was planning to destroy the Babylonians. This ambush would not destroy the Babylonians it would only be a step in Yahweh's plan to destroy Babylon. Let's read this passage so we see it in context.

"Sharpen the arrows, take up the shields! **Yahweh has stirred up the kings of the Medes, because his purpose is to destroy Babylon.** Yahweh will take vengeance, vengeance for his temple. Lift up a banner against the walls of Babylon! Reinforce the guard, station the watchmen, **prepare an ambush!** Yahweh will carry out his purpose, his decree against the people of Babylon. You who live by many waters and are rich in treasures, your end has come, the time for you to be cut off" (Jeremiah 51:11-13).

This ambush of the Babylonians by the Iranians will most likely be the "great battle" mentioned in Revelation's Second Seal prophecy.

"Then another horse came out, a fiery red one. Its rider was given power to take peace from the earth and to make men slay each other. To him was given large sword (**great battle**)" (Revelation 6:4).

Jeremiah was also told what would happen when this Second Seal War began between the U.S. and Iran. As we recall from Habakkuk's chapter two prophecies, the President of the Babylonians will cause incredible death and destruction bringing shame on himself and the United States. This is what Jeremiah said would occur when that happened:

"The sound of **a cry comes from Babylon**, the sound of great destruction from the land of the Babylonians" (Jeremiah 51:54).

I should also point out that the verses before and after this one in Jeremiah helps capture Yahweh's plan for Babylon. Because, as we see, there is nothing the U.S. can do to prevent its defeat and ultimate destruction. Even its missile defenses and 'Star Wars" will not protect her.

"Even if Babylon reaches the sky and fortifies her lofty stronghold, I will send destroyers against her," declares Yahweh. "The sound of a cry comes from Babylon, the sound of great destruction from the land of the Babylonians. Yahweh will destroy Babylon; he will silence her noisy din" (Jeremiah 51:53-55).

Yahweh told Jeremiah all about the Time of the End Babylonians. Not only did Yahweh tell Jeremiah everything, He even used the same wording that He gave John in the Book of Revelation. The similarities between Revelation 17 – 18 and Jeremiah 50 – 51 are another way that Yahweh used to help His people see who the End Time Babylonians are. This information will become a matter of life and death for many of Yahweh's people, those living in the United States of America.

Let's compare some passages from Revelation and Jeremiah so that we can see how God speaks of End Time Babylon. Below are just seven of the numerous examples:

(1) Many Waters:

- "Come, I will show you the punishment of the great prostitute, who sits on many waters." (Revelation 17:1)

- "You who live by many waters and are rich in treasures, your end has come," (Jeremiah 51:13)

(2) Gold Cup:

- "She held a golden cup in her hand, filled with abominable things and the filth of her adulteries." (Revelation 17:4)

- "Babylon was a gold cup in the Lord's hand; she made the whole earth drunk." (Jeremiah 51:7)

(3) Whole World Drunk:

- "All the nations have drunk the maddening wine of her adulteries." (Revelation 18:3)

- "She made the whole earth drunk. The nations drank her wine; therefore they have now gone mad." (Jeremiah 51:7)

(4) Come Out of Her:

- "Come out of her, my people, so that you will not share in her sins, so that you will 'not receive any of her plagues." (Revelation 18:4)

- "Come out of her, my people! Run for your lives! Run from the fierce anger of the LORD." (Jeremiah 51:45)

(5) Consumed by Fire:

- "Therefore in one day her plagues will overtake her: death, mourning and famine. She will be consumed by fire, for mighty is the Lord God who judges her." (Revelation 18:8)

- "Yahweh Almighty says: 'Babylon's thick wall will be leveled and her high gates set on fire; the peoples exhaust themselves for nothing, the nations' labor is only fuel for the flames.'" (Jeremiah 51:58)

(6) In One Day:

- "Therefore in one day her plagues will overtake her: death, mourning and famine. She will be consumed by fire, for mighty is the Lord God who judges her." (Revelation 18:8)

- "For their day has come, the time for them to be punished. ... Therefore, her young men will fall in the streets; all her soldiers will be silenced in that day," declares Yahweh." (Jeremiah 50:27, 30)

(7) The Queen's not eternal:

- "In her heart she boasts, 'I sit as queen; I am not a widow, and I will never mourn.' Therefore in one day her plagues will overtake her:" (Revelation 18:7-8)

- "'I will continue forever--the eternal queen!' But you did not consider these things or reflect on what might happen. Now then, listen, you wanton creature, lounging in your security and saying to yourself, 'I am, and there is none besides me. I will never be a widow or suffer the loss of children.' Both of these will overtake you in a moment, on a single day:" (Isaiah 47:7-8)

These examples combined with the prophecies themselves confirm that Jeremiah 50 and 51 and Revelation 17 and 18 are about the same nation during the Time of the End.

Isaiah has something to say.

Yahweh also spoke to Isaiah about the U.S.A. in the same way. Below are two examples so we can see the similarity.

- "Babylon, the jewel of kingdoms, the glory of the Babylonians' pride, will be **overthrown by God like Sodom and Gomorrah**" (Isaiah 13:19).

- "**As God overthrew Sodom and Gomorrah** along with their neighboring towns," declares Yahweh no one will live there; no man will dwell in it. "Look! An army is coming from the north; a great nation and many kings are being stirred up from the ends of the earth" (Jeremiah 50:40-41).

Yahweh has the same message for His people who live in End Time Babylon as we can see from each of the prophets:

- "**Leave Babylon, flee from the Babylonians**! Announce this with shouts of joy and proclaim it. Send it out to the ends of the earth; say" (Isaiah 48:20).

- **"Flee out of Babylon; leave the land of the Babylonians,** and be like the goats that lead the flock. For I will stir up and bring against Babylon an alliance of great nations from the land of the north" (Jeremiah 50:8-9).

- "Fallen! Fallen is Babylon the Great! She has become a home for demons and a haunt for every evil spirit, a haunt for every unclean and detestable bird. ... **Come out of her, my people,** so that you will not share in her sins, so that you will not receive any of her plagues" (Revelation 18:2, 4).

- "Come, O Zion! Escape, you who live in the Daughter of Babylon!" (Zechariah 2:7)

At this point in our discussion of the Time of the End we have examined the first three prophetic witnesses. These three establish that the "Time of the End Has Come." The three prophetic witnesses are:

1. The First Seal of Revelation.
2. The Second Seal of Revelation.
3. The Prophecies of Habakkuk.

As we have examined these early witnesses to the Time of the End we where able to discover the identity of the End Time Babylonians. This discovery will prove to be critically important to many of God's people as we discuss the Third Seal of Revelation in the next chapter.

We now know:

- Habakkuk the third witness to the End Time.
- The USA to be the End Time Babylonians.
- The President will be taunted by all people and all nations.
- That the United States is definitely in Bible prophecy.

Chapter 7
Rider on the Black Horse

In this chapter we will be examining Revelation's Third Seal horse and rider and discussing why this prophecy is extremely important to God's people, a matter of life and death to many.

When the First Seal opened in 2001, President George W. Bush and the U.S. Military went out conquering in the War on Terror.

When the Second Seal opens, President Mahmoud Ahmadinejad and the Iranian Revolutionary Guard will start World War by ambushing the U.S. Navy. The Second Seal crisis will also fulfill a number of Habakkuk's prophecies and awaken all Bible churches to the Time of the End.

As Birth Pans

Before we examine the red horse and rider of Revelation 6, we should remember that we are considering biblical prophecies that Christ referred to as "birth pains." Birth pains in pregnancy start small and increase in severity. Just as the Second Seal Crisis will be larger than the First, the Third Seal Crisis will be larger than the Second. Also, as birth pains come more quickly as pregnancy progresses, the Third Seal Crisis will follow more quickly than did the Second from the First.

Time between each of the seals will shorten.

First Seal Crisis – Sept. 11, 2001

Second Seal Crisis – 2012 ? (about 10 years)

Third Seal Crisis – Will be less than 10 years.

When Christ opens the third seal it appears that the rider on the black horse will cause damage to the world's supply of wheat and barley. Below, is the Third Seal prophecy.

> "When the Lamb opened **the third seal**, I heard the third living creature say, "Come!" I looked, and there before me was a black horse! **Its rider was holding a pair of scales** in his hand. Then I heard what sounded like a voice among the four living creatures, saying, "A quart of wheat for a day's wages, and three quarts of barley for a day's wages, and do not damage the oil and the wine!" (Revelation 6:5-6)

At least one word in this translation may be worth examining more closely. The Greek word which is translated "**pair of scales**" is "zugos." Zugos; figuratively means to yoke together, a coupling. Literally 'zugos" means a beam of a balance (as connecting scales). Therefore, the rider on the black horse may have something to do with balance in the world, like the balance of power. This seems a likely interpretation because each of the riders on the four horses has something to do with starting a war. Therefore, it may be that this rider will change or alter the balance of power in the world by starting the Third Seal War.

There is another thing in this prophecy that seems to connote war. It says, "do not damage the oil and the wine!" which implies that wheat and barley are damaged which causes a sharp rise in the price of wheat and barley.

Zechariah's Map of the Four Colored Horses

Let's get some geographic perspective of the Black Horse from our world map of the four colored horses below.

RUSSIA

USA

ISRAEL

IRAN

EGYPT

1st Seal: White Horse - USA
2nd Seal: Red Horse - Iran
3rd Seal: Black Horse - Russia

As we can see, Russia is the country north of Israel capable of starting this next End Time War.

Wheat and Barley Damaged

When this war takes place it appears that wheat and barley are damaged causing a dramatic rise in the price of wheat and barley. After the wheat and barley are damaged it will cost a day's wages to buy a day's supply of wheat or barley bread.

Today, the United States of America and Canada combined typically represent the top world exporters of wheat and barley.[4] The USA and Canada together provide about 40% of the global market for wheat exports.

Secondly, Russia has for several years been rebuilding its strategic nuclear capabilities.[5] Some believe that under the leadership of Vladimir Putin, the Russian Bear has awakened and has revived its Cold War strategies.

4

http://www.abareconomics.com/interactive/08_ResearchReports/gmcrops/htm/chapter_3.htm

If Russia attacks the United States, the United States would likely be able to counter attack and cause significant devastation to Russia. Russia also is a major producer of wheat. Therefore, if Russia were to engage the U.S. in a thermo nuclear war, wheat and barley would very likely reach the cost described in the Third Seal prophecy.

Babylon the Great a.k.a. the U.S.A.

We have already begun our examination of the End Time Babylonians in the last chapter. But, now in light of the Third Seal horse and rider we need to take a closer look at these End Time Babylonians. We must be absolutely certain that the Babylonians are none other than the United States of America.

We must be certain because God has commanded that His people flee from the land of the Babylonians before she is attacked. Since it appears that Russia is the nation from the north that will attack the U.S.A. we should also be able to confirm this prophetic fact in other prophecies about End Time Babylon. Because of the critical nature of Babylon's identity for God's people, we would be wise to apply the "two or three witnesses to establish a matter" rule.

Since Jeremiah wrote extensively about the End Time Babylonians we will start with his prophecies. According to Jeremiah who is it that will attack the Babylonians? What does Yahweh say?

> "This is the word Yahweh spoke through Jeremiah the prophet concerning Babylon and the land of the Babylonians: Announce and proclaim among the nations, lift up a banner and proclaim it; keep nothing back,... **A nation from the north will attack her** and lay waste her land" (Jeremiah 50:1-3).

This next passage from Jeremiah seems to capture several important aspects concerning Babylon's defeat including God's command for His people to flee from Babylon.

[5] http://online.wsj.com/article/SB121928439171059051.html?mod=googlenews_wsj

> "**Flee out of Babylon;** leave the land of the Babylonians, and be like the goats that lead the flock. For I will stir up and bring against Babylon **an alliance of great nations from the land of the north.** They will take up their positions against her, and **from the north** she will be captured. Their arrows will be like skilled warriors who do not return empty-handed. So Babylonia will be plundered" (Jeremiah 50:8-10).

Yahweh tells us that End Time Babylon will be defeated by fire in a moment by a nation from the north along with an alliance of other nations. It's also interesting that this destruction comes as "their arrows will be like skilled warriors." Arrows are weapons of war that fly through the air. In ancient times it was the archers that were the skilled warriors. Today ICBM's are programmed to operate like skilled warriors and evade detection and interception by antimissile missile systems.

> "**As God overthrew Sodom and Gomorrah** along with their neighboring towns," declares Yahweh, "so no one will live there; no man will dwell in it. "Look! **An army is coming from the north**; a **great nation and many kings** are being stirred up from the ends of the earth" (Jeremiah 50:40-41).

From history, we know that these prophecies are not about ancient Babylon. Ancient Babylon gradually faded away over many decades. She was not destroyed by fire in one hour as End Time Babylon will be. Let's confirm this one day and one hour destruction by fire with some other prophetic witnesses before we move on. Here what Isaiah wrote about End Time Babylon:

> "**Babylon,** the jewel of kingdoms, the glory of the Babylonians' pride, **will be overthrown by God like Sodom and Gomorrah**" (Isaiah 13:19).

John also wrote of the destruction of End Time Babylon in the Book of Revelation.

"The beast [Antichrist] and the ten horns you saw will hate the prostitute. They will bring her to ruin and leave her naked; they will eat her flesh and **burn her with fire**. For God has put it into their hearts to accomplish his purpose" (Revelation 17:16-17).

"Therefore **in one day** her plagues will overtake her: death, mourning and famine. **She will be consumed by fire**, for mighty is the Lord God who judges her. "When the kings of the earth who committed adultery with her and shared her luxury see the smoke of her burning, they will weep and mourn over her. Terrified at her torment, they will stand far off and cry: "'Woe! Woe, O great city, O Babylon, city of power! **In one hour your doom has come**!' "The merchants of the earth will weep and mourn over her because **no one** buys their cargoes any more" (Revelation 18:8-11).

How End Time Babylon is destroyed is no mystery! When the US is destroyed by fire in one day and one hour the world wide economy stops because the world's great consumer nation is gone. What other nation could possibly cause "The merchants of the earth will weep and mourn over her because **no one** buys their cargoes any more"?

But, what about the wheat and barley destruction mentioned in the Third Seal prophecy? Do we see anything about this when the Land of the Babylonians is destroyed? Jeremiah says this about that.

"Cut off from Babylon the sower, and the reaper with his sickle at harvest" (Jeremiah 50:16).

"Come against her from afar. Break open her granaries; pile her up like heaps of grain. Completely destroy her and leave her no remnant" (Jeremiah 50:26).

Are We Awake Yet?

Hopefully, by now, everyone is seeing why Yahweh is telling His people to leave the land of the End Time Babylonians before it is too late.

Yahweh's warning for His people to "**come out**" was one of the reasons I was able to see that the "Parable of the Ten Virgins" awakening happened as a result of the Second Seal War. I reasoned that if there was any hope of God's people getting the message to leave Babylon before its destruction, His people would have to be awake for some time before that happened.

In the Matthew 25 parable, there are a couple of clues that alert us to the fact that the awakening of the "ten virgins" is before Babylon's destruction at the Third Seal War.

The first clue:

At the time of the parable, Christ said the virgins were told to "**come out**" to meet Him.

> "At midnight the cry rang out: 'See, the bridegroom is coming! "**Come out**" (exerchomai) to meet him!' Then all the virgins woke up" (Matthew 25:6-7).

The word in the Greek translated "**come out**" is "exerchomai."

> Exerchomai means to come out, depart (out of), escape, get out, go (abroad, away, out).

This same word is used in exactly the same context in Christ's warning to His people in Revelation 18:4 as we read below regarding "Babylon the Great."

> "**Come out** (exerchomai) of her, my people, so that you will not share in her sins, so that you will not receive any of her plagues" (Revelation 18:4).

The Second Clue:

At the time of the parable a great cry is heard.

"At midnight **the cry rang out**: 'See, the bridegroom is coming! "Come out to meet him!' Then all the virgins woke up" (Matthew 25:6-7).

That cry, at the time of the Second Seal War, is the same cry that Jeremiah said would come from the Babylonians.

> "**The sound of a cry** comes from Babylon, the sound of great destruction from the land of the Babylonians. Yahweh will destroy Babylon; ... A destroyer will come against Babylon" (Jeremiah 51:54-56).

When Yahweh's people wake up and turn to the Bible, they will see why they must "come out" of Babylon before it is too late. This may be a good time to take another look at our timeline and the 2nd Seal.

Time of the End: 3rd Seal

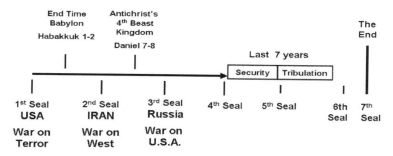

Therefore, soon after the Second Seal is opened, Yahweh's people will begin to see their need to leave Babylon before the Third Seal is opened. **Then two questions will arise**.

When to leave and where do we go?

Since we know that Christ has told us everything ahead of time, we will seek the answers to our two questions in Scripture.

1) When to Leave Babylon?

Since the Second Seal War has already awakened God's people, should they leave immediately?

The short answer is that we each leave when we are led by the Spirit of God to leave. However, God also gives us the information we need from Scripture to help make that decision.

We know that we must leave before the Third Seal opens and Russia and her allies attack the U.S.A. But, how do we know when to leave, are there any prerequisites to the attack on the Babylonians?

Yes, a few.

Antichrist – Master of Intrigue

Because this question is a matter of life and death, I am going to give the correct answer first. The correct answer is that you must not trust in Man, you must put you life and faith in Yahweh alone and do what He tells you.

Now, I will tell you what Yahweh has revealed to me about the when His people must be out of Babylon and the "Land of the Babylonians."

Bible prophecy reveals in both Daniel and Revelation who is behind the destruction of Babylon, a.k.a. the U.S.A. Today, the USA is considered the only Superpower. But by the time of the Third Seal War, others like China and Russia will be considered to be superpowers as well. Because the term superpower is foreign to biblical terminology we must look to see how Scripture expresses the idea of a superpower. Here Daniel calls the End Time superpowers, "**mighty men**" and he identifies the person behind their destruction as the "stern-faced king, a master of intrigue" which we call the Antichrist.

"In the latter part of their reign, when rebels have become completely wicked, a stern-faced king (Antichrist), a master of intrigue, will arise. **He will become very strong, but not by his own power**. He will cause astounding devastation and will succeed in whatever he does. **He will destroy the mighty men**" (Daniel 8:23-24).

Notice that the Antichrist accomplishes the destruction of the superpowers, "**not by his own power**." From what we have already learned about the Black Horse and the nation from the north, we could conclude that the "master of intrigue" will convince Russia to attack the U.S.A. If that were to happen then the US would counter attack and two superpowers would be destroyed – "He will destroy the mighty men."

Daniel addresses the defeat of the superpowers by the Antichrist two times in his prophecies. Here is the second time and he calls the superpowers, "the mightiest fortresses."

"He (Antichrist) will attack the **mightiest fortresses** with the help of a **foreign god** and will greatly honor those who acknowledge him" (Daniel 11:39).

Once again Daniel tells us that the Antichrist accomplishes the destruction of the superpowers "**with the help of a foreign god**" or as we might say today, with the help of a foreign power. Russia, for example.

From Daniel's prophecies we can determine that the Antichrist is behind the destruction of the superpowers, including the USA. But what did John say in the book of Revelation? He also indicated that the Beast King known as Antichrist would be responsible for Babylon's fiery destruction in one day and one hour. Here is what John wrote:

> "**The beast (Antichrist) and the ten horns** you saw will
> hate the prostitute. They **will bring her to ruin** and leave her
> naked; they will eat her flesh **and burn her with fire**. For
> God has put it into their hearts to accomplish his purpose"
> (Revelation 17:16-17).

> "Therefore **in one day** her plagues will overtake her: death,
> mourning and famine. **She will be consumed by fire**, for
> mighty is the Lord God who judges her" (Revelation 18:8).

The Antichrist a.k.a. the Beast from the Middle East will be
responsible for the destruction of the USA.

When will this Happen?

When will the Antichrist come to power and be in a position to
convince Russia and others to attack the US? Once again Daniel and
Revelation have the answer. Daniel is the one who detailed the rise
of the Antichrist from a ten nation Middle-eastern kingdom. Here is
what God told Daniel,

> "He gave me this explanation: 'The fourth beast is a fourth
> kingdom that will appear on earth. It will be different from
> all the other kingdoms and will devour the whole earth,
> trampling it down and crushing it. **The ten horns are ten
> kings** who will come from this kingdom. After them **another
> king will arise**, different from the earlier ones; he will
> subdue three kings" (Daniel 7:23-24).

From Daniel chapter seven we learn that the ten nation Middle-
eastern kingdom will come together first and then the Antichrist will
rise from among the ten. I believe the Antichrist will become the
new leader of Iraq, possibly even the next leader of Iraq after Prime
Minister Nouri al-Maliki.

When the Antichrist takes his position as one of the 10 kings of the
"fourth beast kingdom" then he will cause astounding devastation
including the destruction of the superpowers.

Revelation reveals that the Antichrist will accomplish this destruction before he subdues the three kings mentioned in Daniel 7:24. Notice in Revelation's prophecy that all ten kings are involved in bringing Babylon to ruin.

> **"The beast (Antichrist) and the ten horns** you saw will hate the prostitute. They **will bring her to ruin** and leave her naked; they will eat her flesh **and burn her with fire"** (Revelation 17:16).

The prophets are telling God's people that they must flee from Babylon as soon as they see "the little horn" (Antichrist) of Daniel 7 take his position among the 10 kings of the Fourth Beast kingdom.

Will the Real Antichrist Stand Up?

What happens if more than one king arises to power among the ten kings, how will we know who the Antichrist is? Once again, let's see what the Bible has to say. In addition to what we already know from Scripture - what other characteristics can we find about the Antichrist?

Where's He From?

Daniel tells us who the ancestors of the Antichrist where. They were the ancient Syrians who were part of General Titus' Roman Army in 70 A.D. They were the people who destroyed the city of Jerusalem and the Jewish Temple. Let's examine how Daniel explained who the people of the Antichrist would be.

> "The people **of the ruler who will come** will destroy the city and the sanctuary." (Daniel 9:26)

We know that "the ruler who will come" is the Antichrist, because the next verse in Daniel details his actions during the last seven years, before the End. Here is what it says about him:

"**He [Antichrist] will** confirm a covenant with many for one 'seven.' In the middle of the 'seven' **he will** put an end to sacrifice and offering. And on a wing of the temple **he will** set up an abomination that causes desolation, until the end that is decreed is poured out on **him**." (Daniel 9:27)

From these verses we can positively identify the Antichrist as "**the ruler who will come**" the "**he**" of Daniel 9:27.

From history we can identify "The people" who "will destroy the city and the sanctuary" of Daniel 9:26. They were the people of the Roman Army in 70 A.D. under the leadership of the Roman General Titus.

This is where many Bible teachers have made a "Big Mistake." They assume that the people in the Roman army were Roman soldiers. But that is not what history recorded.

Fortunately, this part of Israel's history was extremely well documented. The Jewish historian, Josephus recorded the details of this time while he was in the employment of the Romans.

Josephus described how General Titus had given orders **NOT** to destroy the Jewish sanctuary, desiring that it remain as a trophy of his victory[6]. Never-the-less, when the final battle was being fought, fire got into the temple and burned the gold covered woodwork. In the heat of the fire the gold melted down into the cracks of the stonework.

Following the battle, the soldiers took down every stone to get at the gold which had melted into the stonework of the temple. This event is another amazing record of how precise God's prophecies are fulfilled. Here is what Christ prophesied about this, 38 years earlier.

---

[6] Josephus: The Complete Works – Wars of the Jews 6.4.3

"Some of his disciples were remarking about how the temple was adorned with beautiful stones and with gifts dedicated to God. But Jesus said, "As for what you see here, the time will come when **not one stone will be left on another; every one of them will be thrown down.**" (Luke 21:5-6)

Josephus also recorded who the soldiers where in Titus' army, the people responsible for the destruction of the city and sanctuary. He wrote that they were Syrians. Syria at that time was part of the Roman Empire and it encompassed present day Syria and Lebanon. Josephus also recorded that following Titus' campaign in Israel, the Syrian soldiers returned home with their loot (gold). At that time the price of gold in Syria dropped in half, due to the amount gold brought home by the Syrian soldiers[7].

From Josephus' historical account we can see that the people who destroyed the city and the sanctuary where ancient Syrians.

Therefore, "the ruler who will come," the Antichrist will be of ancient Syrian descent. The territory of Ancient Syria is today Lebanon and Syria. Therefore, the Antichrist's ancestors will be from either Lebanon or Syria.

There are many prophecies which point to the Middle East as the place where the Antichrist will arise to power.

The Beast from the Middle East

Let's examine Scripture to see what Yahweh says about where the Antichrist will be from and over what counties he will rule.

---

[7] Josephus: The Complete Works – Wars of the Jews 6.6.1

Daniel's prophecies indicate that the fourth kingdom arises from the area of the first three Middle East kingdoms; Babylon, Media-Persia and Greece. Even Alexander's kingdom was centered in the Middle East. After Alexander the Great conquered the known world from Greece to India, he returned to Babylon and governed from there. Alexander's capital Babylon was located on the Euphrates River south of present day Baghdad in Iraq.

Now, let's look at a prophecy which directly identifies the ancient area and nation from where the Antichrist will rule. The prophet Isaiah wrote about the Antichrist and described his Time of the End exploits. Here is one of my favorite examples of how Isaiah identifies where the Antichrist will be from.

In chapter ten of Isaiah, Isaiah describes that the Time of the End Assyrian king will come against Israel. This passage below describes that the surviving remnant of Israel will at first rely on the Antichrist. Then the Antichrist will strike them down until the end. Finally, the remnant of Israel will truly rely on Yahweh. Here is how that is recorded:

> "In that day the remnant of Israel, the survivors of the house of Jacob, will no longer **rely on him** [King of Assyria] **who struck them down** but will truly **rely on Yahweh**, the Holy One of Israel." (Isaiah 10:20)

We know that the "King of Assyria" is the Antichrist, because Isaiah's description matches perfectly with Daniel's description about the Antichrist. Here is Daniel's version:

> **"He [Antichrist] will confirm a covenant** with many for one 'seven.' In the middle of the 'seven' **he will put an end to sacrifice and offering**. And on a wing of the temple he will set up an abomination that causes desolation, **until the end"** (Daniel 9:27)

In Daniel's prophecy the Antichrist will at first confirm a peace treaty with Israel. Israel will rely on him. Then after 3.5 years he will break the treaty at the time of the "abomination that causes desolation". Then he will "strike them down" (persecute them) during the Great Tribulation, until the Messiah returns at the end of the age and saves His people from the Antichrist. Then they will truly rely on the Messiah, the Holy One of Israel.

In both prophecies the Antichrist will at first cause Israel to rely on him. Then later he will beat them down during the Great Tribulation. At the end of the age, Yahweh will return and Israel will then rely on Him. Connecting these two key Time of the End prophecies, we can see that the Assyrian King is the Antichrist.

The prophet Isaiah was not the only prophet to identify the ruler who will come against Israel at the Time of the End. Micah also referred to the Antichrist as the Assyrian, as we see here:

> "He [Messiah] will stand and shepherd his flock in the strength of Yahweh, in the majesty of the name of Yahweh his God. And they [Israel] will live securely, for then his greatness will reach to the ends of the earth. And he will be their peace. When **the Assyrian** invades our land" (Micah 5:4-5)

The prophet Zephaniah also wrote of Assyria as being the kingdom which will come against Israel during the Time of the End. Zephaniah further identified Assyria by referring to the Assyrian city of Nineveh. We can also be sure that this prophecy is about the end and Yahweh's return, because Yahweh says "wait for me" and that the "whole world will be consumed by the fire". Let's read the prophecy:

"He will stretch out his hand against the north and **destroy Assyria, leaving Nineveh utterly desolate** and dry as the desert.... 'Therefore wait for me,' declares Yahweh, for the day I will stand up to testify. I have decided to assemble the nations, to gather the kingdoms and to pour out my wrath on them-- all my fierce anger. The whole world will be consumed by the fire of my jealous anger." (Zephaniah 2:13, 3:8)

The prophet Nahum, like Zephaniah, referred to the city of Nineveh as the place of the Antichrist. Also like Zephaniah, Nahum indicates that Yahweh will totally destroy Nineveh in the end, as we read below:

"From you, O Nineveh, has one come Fourth who plots evil against Yahweh and counsels wickedness. This is what Yahweh says: 'Although they have allies and are numerous, they will be cut off and pass away. Although I have afflicted you, O Judah, I will afflict you no more.' ... Yahweh has given a command concerning you, Nineveh: 'You will have no descendants to bear your name.'" (Nahum 1:11-14)

From what the prophets have written, we can see for ourselves that the Antichrist will come from the land of ancient Assyria. **Ancient Assyria is present day Iraq**. Therefore, we need to keep a close watch on Iraq as we wait for the Antichrist and his kingdom to appear and then begin its rise to world power.

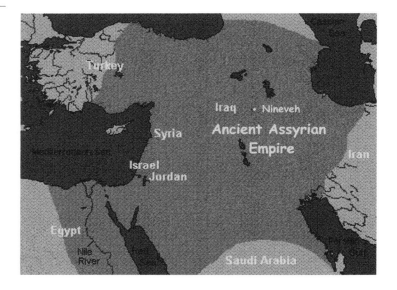

We are also told that the King of Assyria, Antichrist, will be successful until Yahweh returns. When the Lord returns He will destroy the Antichrist who fought against Jerusalem, as we read here:

> "When the Lord has finished all his work against Mount Zion and Jerusalem, he will say, 'I will punish the king of Assyria [Antichrist] for the willful pride of his heart and the haughty look in his eyes.'" (Isaiah 10:12)

Now, we know that the Antichrist will come from present day Iraq. What else do we need to know about him?

What does Antichrist look like?

In Isaiah's passage above that we were told something about the Assyrian King's appearance. He has a haughty or proud look in his eyes. This is not the only place in prophecy that gives us an indication of the Antichrist's appearance. Here are two others examples from Daniel's prophecies:

"I also wanted to know about ... the horn [Antichrist] that **looked more imposing [stout] than the others and that had eyes** and a mouth **that spoke boastfully**." (Daniel 7:20)

"In the latter part of their reign, when rebels have become completely wicked, a **stern-faced king**," (Daniel 8:23)

This is what we know about the Antichrist's appearance:

- He has a haughty or a proud look in his eyes.
- He looks more imposing than the other 9 kings.
- He has eyes that speak boastfully.
- He is a stern-faced king.

What else do we need to know?

Antichrist Is Like

In addition to what we have already learned from Scripture, what else do the prophets say about the Beast King we call Antichrist?

Here are a few brief descriptions and their scriptural references.

The Antichrist will:

- Try to change the set times and the laws – Daniel 7:25
- Be a master of intrigue – Daniel 8:23
- Cause astounding devastation - Daniel 8:24
- Succeed in whatever he does – Daniel 8:24
- Cause deceit to prosper - Daniel 8:25
- Corrupt with flattery – Daniel 11:32
- Have no regard for the gods of his fathers – Daniel 11:37
- Greatly honor those who acknowledge him – Daniel 11:39
- Purpose to destroy – Isaiah 10:7
- Put an end to many nations – Isaiah 10:7

As we can see from these descriptions the Antichrist will not be a Christ like figure. Even though he will confirm a peace treaty, he will not be a peace maker. He will rule the whole world but he will not be the head of a mythical "One World Government" or a "New World Order" as some people imagine. The Antichrist will be a military ruler and a destroyer of nations.

These biblical prophecies help us understand about the Antichrist and his Middle-eastern kingdom with its 7 heads and 10 horns. Armed with this information we will have little difficulty identifying this fourth kingdom and the Antichrist when they soon appear on the world scene.

We are over 10 years into the Time of the End. Following the Second Seal and the start of World War III - the next prophecies to be fulfilled will deal with the rise of the Antichrist. Therefore, today, the Antichrist is alive and well and from Iraq.

For hundreds of years people have tried unsuccessfully to identify who the Antichrist would be. But, now that we are so close to the fulfillment of these prophecies about the Antichrist, perhaps we should take a look around to see if there is anyone who currently meets the criteria and characteristics which have been prophesied.

First let's list the characteristics of the Antichrist.

Characteristics of the Antichrist:

- **Ancestry**: Ancient Syria which is present day Lebanon, Syria and parts of southern Turkey.

- **National ruler**: Ancient Assyria which is present day Iraq.

- **Personal Character**: A military leader who will honor a god of fortress.

- **Physical Characteristics**: Stern-faced, haughty look, stout, more imposing than his peers.

There is one Middle-eastern Iraqi leader who meets some of the qualifications of the Antichrist. He is also, potentially, in a position to become the future leader of Iraq. That person is **Sayyid Muqtadā al-Sadr**. Let's compare him to the characteristics of the Antichrist and determine if he is the man.

Muqtada al-Sadr:

- **Ancestry**: Muqtada al-Sadr is of **Lebanese** ancestry.

- **National ruler**: Muqtada al-Sadr was born in Baghdad, Iraq. He is currently living in Iran where he became an **Ayatollah**. He is one of the most influential religious and political figures in Iraq. "Senior British officers were of the opinion that the radical cleric Muqtada al-Sadr, the leader of the Shia Mahdi Army, would enter the political process"[8] which he has.

- **Personal Character**: Muqtada al-Sadr is the founder and leader of the 60,000 man Mahdi Army in Iraq.

- **Physical Characteristics**: Muqtada al-Sadr is stern-faced, has a haughty look, and is stout and more imposing than other Middle-eastern leaders.

If Muqtada al-Sadr becomes the future leader of Iraq, he will also become the Antichrist. Newsweek magazine called him the most dangerous man in Iraq.

---

[8] http://www.independent.co.uk/news/uk/politics/british-troops-to-start-iraq-pullout-in-march-1059445.html

106

If Muqtada al-Sadr fulfills the prophecies of the Antichrist, he will become the most dangerous man in the world.

What We Know About the Antichrist

- The Fourth Kingdom comes **before** the Antichrist.
- His ancestors will be from Lebanon or Syria.
- His Kingdom will include present day Iraq.
- He will cause the devastation of the USA.

Therefore, when the Antichrist joins the ten nation Middle-eastern kingdom, God's people need to leave End Time Babylon.

2) Where Do We Go?

The next question to ask Yahweh is this; where do we go when we leave the Land of the Babylonians?

To this question Yahweh has two answers; one for His people and one for everyone else. First, let's read the answer for everyone else.

"Cut off from Babylon the sower, and the reaper with his sickle at harvest. Because of the sword of the oppressor let everyone return to his own people, let **everyone flee to his own land**" (Jeremiah 50:16).

However, Yahweh's instructions for His people are more specific. Here are three of the six examples from Jeremiah 50 and 51 where Yahweh tells His people where to go when they flee from Babylon.

"In those days, at that time," declares Yahweh, "the people of Israel and the people of Judah together will go in tears to seek Yahweh their God. **They will ask the way to Zion** and turn their faces toward it. They will come and bind themselves to Yahweh in an everlasting covenant" (Jeremiah 50:4-5).

"Listen to the fugitives and **refugees from Babylon declaring in Zion** how Yahweh our God has taken vengeance, vengeance for his temple" (Jeremiah 50:28).

"Yahweh has vindicated us; come, let us tell **in Zion** what Yahweh our God has done" (Jeremiah 51:10).

Yahweh is telling His people to flee Babylon before her destruction and go to Israel for the duration of the Time of the End. That simple sounding exodus of God's people will be extremely difficult. Therefore, it seems that Yahweh has planned to encourage His people home to Israel.

Yahweh Entices His People Home

Scripture does not provide the timing of these next prophecies. However, I believe that at least some of these will happen in Israel before the Third Seal is opened. The fulfillment of each of these prophecies will tend to convince Yahweh's people, both Hebrew and Gentile that "The Time Has Come" to return home in preparation for the Coming Messiah.

The prophecies that are certain to be fulfilled are about the rebuilding of the Temple and a future peace covenant with Israel. However, Scripture does not provide, nor do we need to know just when these events will happen. We know that they will happen and we will recognize them when they do. Let's look at the future temple first.

Third Jewish Temple

Daniel indicates that Yahweh's Temple will exist on the Temple Mount in the middle of the last seven years – the 70th 'seven' of Daniel chapter nine.

> "He [Antichrist] will confirm a covenant with many for one 'seven.' **In the middle of the 'seven'** he will put an end to sacrifice and offering. And on a wing of **the temple** he will set up an abomination that causes desolation, until the end that is decreed is poured out on him" (Daniel 9:27).

The apostle Paul also indicated that the Temple would be in existence at the time of the "abomination that causes desolation" when he described that situation this way.

> "He [Antichrist] will oppose and will exalt himself over everything that is called God or is worshiped, so that he sets himself up **in God's temple**, proclaiming himself to be God" (2 Thessalonians 2:4).

We know when Yahweh's Temple will exist on the Temple Mount. However, there is no indication in Scripture when the temple will be built.

Peace in the Middle East

In Daniel's passage above we are also told that the Antichrist will "confirm a covenant" at the beginning of the last seven years. This means that there will already be a covenant in existence at that time when the Antichrist will put his weight behind it. It will not be a covenant that he makes; he'll confirm one that already exists.

Scripture does not indicate when the initial covenant will be made. However, I feel strongly that it will be made sometime between the second and third seals of Revelation.

What else could happen?

Raiders of the lost Ark

These next relatively small End Time prophecies could also play a very large role in Yahweh's plan to get His people home for the Holy days. These are some of the prophetic passages that seem to indicate that the ancient tabernacle of Moses, the one that went through the desert with the Israelites, will be discovered soon.

> "I will give the command, and I will shake the house of Israel among all the nations as grain is shaken in a sieve, and not a pebble will reach the ground. All the sinners among my people will die by the sword, all those who say, 'Disaster will not overtake or meet us.' In that day **I will restore David's fallen tent**. I will repair its broken places, restore its ruins, and build it **as it used to be, ... I will bring back my exiled people Israel**" (Amos 9:9-14).

> " I am Yahweh your God, who brought you out of Egypt; I will make you live in tents again, as in the days of your appointed feasts. ... Do they sacrifice bulls **in Gilgal? Their altars will be like piles of stones on a plowed field**" (Hosea 12:9/11).

Since King David did not build a temple for Yahweh, he worshiped using Moses tent. If this prophecy speaks to that tent then we can expect that the tabernacle and the "Ark of the Covenant" to be discovered before Yahweh's Temple is built on the Temple Mount. Also as indicated in the Hosea prophecy, when they are found they will be set up again in Gilgal and the Israelites will once again live in tents as they use the ancient tabernacle (tent of David) to worship as they did during Exodus.

We definitely have some interesting biblical history to review as we anticipate the discoveries soon to take place.

What we now know:

- Russia is the Black Horse of the Third Seal.
- President Putin will be the rider on the black horse.
- The U.S.A. is End Time Babylon.
- The Antichrist is behind Babylon's Destruction.
- We leave before the Third Seal.
- God's people must go to Israel.

Chapter 8
Rider on the Pale Horse

In this chapter we will be examining Revelation's Fourth Seal horse and rider and discussing why this prophecy is important to God's people.

The First Seal opened on 9/11 in 2001, and then President George W. Bush and the U.S. Military went out conquering in the War on Terror.

When the Second Seal opens, possibly in 2012, President Mahmoud Ahmadinejad and the Iranian Revolutionary Guard will start World War by ambushing the U.S. Navy. This Second Seal crisis will also begin to fulfill a number of Habakkuk's prophecies and awaken all Bible churches to the Time of the End.

When the Messiah opens the Third Seal, President Vladimir Putin and the Russia Military will launch a nuclear attack on the USA, destroying her as a nation. The USA will likely counter attack severely damaging Russia and possibly China as well.

Now we are going to examine the pale horse and rider of Revelation's Fourth Seal. There are several other prophecies that will also be fulfilled at the time of the Fourth Seal. These prophecies will positively identify the pale horse country and when this War will occur.

Fourth Seal Related Prophecies Will:

- Identify the Pale Horse country by name.
- Indicate when the Antichrist subdues the 3 Kings.
- Take place at the beginning of the last seven years.
- When Antichrist confirms a covenant.

Let's start by examining the horse and rider of the Fourth Seal.

> "I looked, and there before me was a pale horse! Its rider was named Death, and Hades was following close behind him. They were given power over a fourth of the earth to kill by sword, famine and plague, and by the wild beasts of the earth" (Revelation 6:8).

As we consider this Fourth Seal prophecy there are several things that we need to keep in mind. First, where to look for the pale horse and rider? Let's start with Zechariah's Map of the Four Colored Horses.

The Four Colored Horses of Zechariah 6

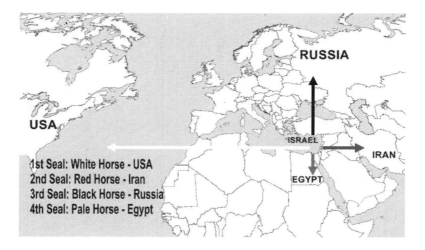

South of Israel is Egypt and the continent of Africa. That is where we need to be watching as we wait for the Fourth Seal War to start.

A second thing we need to keep in mind is that this will be the Fourth Time of the End "birth pain." Which means, like the other birth pains, this war will come quickly after the Third Seal war and it will be more severe than any of the three previous wars we have discussed. The idea that this will be a bigger war seems to be born out by the prophecy itself when it says, "They were given power over a fourth of the earth to kill by sword, famine and plague, and by the wild beasts of the earth." Whether "a fourth of the earth" refers to land mass or population, we can see that this war will be very large indeed.

Remember how we used other End Time prophecies to confirm that the Third Seal black horse from the north symbolized Russia? Let's do the same with the pale horse from the south to see what Yahweh says. What End Time prophecies correspond to the Fourth Seal War? The prophet Daniel has a prophecy that tells us several things about the Fourth Seal war. Let's see what we can learn from Daniel chapter eleven.

The King of the South

The first thing we see in Daniel 11:39 is that the Antichrist attacks "the mightiest fortresses." As we learned in the last chapter regarding Rider on the Black Horse, this is when the Third Seal was opened and the US is destroyed as a nation.

After that the king of the South, Egypt engages the Antichrist in battle. The king of the South is the Fourth Seal rider on the pale horse. Therefore, the timing of this war in Daniel chapter eleven is after the Third Seal and it corresponds exactly with the Fourth Seal war we are considering.

"He [Antichrist] will attack **the mightiest fortresses** with the help of a foreign god and will greatly honor those who acknowledge him. ... At the time of the end the **king of the South** will engage him [Antichrist] in battle, and the king of the North will storm out against him with chariots and cavalry and a great fleet of ships. He [Antichrist] will invade many countries and sweep through them like a flood. He [Antichrist] will also invade the Beautiful Land. ... He [Antichrist] will extend his power over many countries; Egypt will not escape. He [Antichrist] will gain control of the treasures of gold and silver and all the riches of Egypt, with the Libyans and Nubians in submission" (Daniel 11:39-43).

There are still a couple more very interesting things revealed in this prophecy that we need to know.

After "the king of the South" (Egypt) engages the Antichrist in battle, the Antichrist "invades the Beautiful Land" (Israel). We know that Israel is "the Beautiful Land" from Daniel 11:16 which is a prophecy that was fulfilled about 200 B.C. in a battle between Antiochus III and Ptolemy V Epiphanies.

Antichrist in Israel

This prophecy places the Antichrist in Israel after the Fourth Seal war. By this time there will have already been a covenant made for Israel's peace. It is very likely that at this time the Antichrist will want to regroup and consolidate his power following the huge war he has just been fighting. Therefore, rather than engage Israel in battle, he will decide to confirm the existing covenant with them and return home to Iraq. This will mark the beginning of the last seven years, the 70th 'seven' of Daniel chapter nine.

"He [Antichrist] will confirm a covenant with many for one 'seven.' In the middle of the 'seven' he will put an end to sacrifice and offering. And on a wing of the temple he will set up an abomination that causes desolation" (Daniel 9:27).

There is still more. Daniel's prophecy names three of the 10 nations that will initially comprise the Kingdom of the Antichrist. Two of the nations have remained to this day while the third is identified by the name of its ancient tribe. Therefore, three of the ten nations will be Egypt, Libya and Sudan. The ancient Nubians were from the territory of Sudan.[9]

> "Egypt, with the Libyans and Nubians **[three] in submission**" (Daniel 11:43).

Not only is this an amazing revelation about three of the ten nations of the Antichrist's kingdom, but it has further confirmation in two of Daniel's earlier prophecies. In Daniel chapter seven, he described how the Kingdom of the Antichrist would arise to power. Let's look at the connection between these three nations named in Daniel eleven and the Daniel seven prophecy below.

> "The fourth beast is a fourth kingdom that will appear on earth. It will be different from all the other kingdoms and will devour the whole earth, trampling it down and crushing it. The ten horns are ten kings who will come from this kingdom. After them another king [Antichrist] will arise, different from the earlier ones; **he will subdue three kings**" (Daniel 7:23-24).

Yahweh also told Daniel about this breakup of the Kingdom of the Antichrist in Daniel chapter two. Let's read what Daniel wrote:

---

[9] http://en.wikipedia.org/wiki/Nubia

"**Finally, there will be a fourth kingdom,** strong as iron--
for iron breaks and smashes everything--and as iron breaks
things to pieces, so **it will crush and break all the others**.
Just as you saw that the feet and toes were partly of baked
clay and partly of iron, so this will be a divided kingdom; yet
it will have some of the strength of iron in it, even as you saw
iron mixed with clay. As the toes were partly iron and partly
clay, so **this kingdom will be partly strong and partly
brittle**. And just as you saw the iron mixed with baked clay,
so the people will be a mixture **and will not remain united**,
any more than iron mixes with clay" (Daniel 2:40-43).

Now we know that the Middle Eastern Kingdom of the Antichrist
will break up when the Fourth Seal is opened. Let's take a look at
our timeline to see where we will be when this happens.

Time of the End: 4ᵗʰ Seal

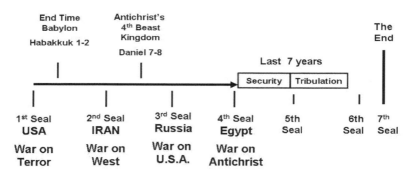

Some of you may be aware that this prophetic revelation about the
Fourth Seal coming at the beginning of the last seven years is a new
interpretation. We should not be surprised by this, because Yahweh
had already told us that this would happen.

Unsealed and Opened at the appointed Time

We should not be surprised by this fact, because Yahweh had already told us as much in His Word. In the Torah Yahweh warned His people about the Time of the End and indicated that He was keeping some prophecy in reserve for that Time of the End. Here is what Yahweh said over 3,500 years ago.

> "They are a nation without sense, there is no discernment in them. If only they were wise and would understand this and discern what their **end will be**! ... Have I not **kept this in reserve** and <u>sealed</u> it in my vaults?" (Deuteronomy 32:28-34)

Daniel also received a similar message from Yahweh indicating that the word about the Time of the End would be sealed until the Time of the End had come. Here is what Yahweh told Daniel.

> "Go your way, Daniel, because the words are closed up and **sealed until the time of the end**" (Daniel 12:9).

Now, that the Time has come, it should not be surprising to us that Revelation's Seals are revealing what has been "**sealed**" – new information that has been hidden in plain sight all this time.

Christ also said something that fits this exactly when He was telling His disciples about the Time of the End. He indicated that no one would be able to know when the Time of the End was going to begin. Christ said,

> "Watch out that you are not deceived. For many will come in my name, claiming, 'I am he,' and, **'The time is near**.' Do not follow them" (Luke 21:8).

No one could possibly have known what the First Seal prophecy meant until after it was opened and unsealed by the Messiah. Then, and only then, would God's people be able to recognize that the First Seal prophecy had been fulfilled and that "The Time Has Come."

My third book, "The Time Has Come: Our Journey Begins".

That is why I say, **"The time is not near, it's here**!" Of course, once "the Time" has come, the End is near. This is another example of the precision of God's Word and why we must read it carefully. It's also the reason that God says this about His Word.

"Do not go beyond what is written" (1 Corinthians 4:6).

Let's review something else before we move on. We have read the Seal prophecies and we are now beginning to grasp what Christ meant when He said,

> **"Be on your guard. I have told you everything ahead of time"**
> (Mark 13:23).

So, what else has the Messiah told us ahead of time that we need to know?

Fourth Beast Kingdom: Ten Kings

We know three of the ten nations that will form the Kingdom of the Antichrist; Egypt, Libya and Sudan. What does Scripture tell us about the other seven? Who will they be?

As of February 2012 the ten nations have not yet come together. They will come together shortly after the Second Seal is opened. When that happens we will see the first part of Daniel 7:24 fulfilled.

We know from the prophecies we discussed, in Chapter 7: The Rider on the Black Horse that the Antichrist will arise out of Iraq.

Ezekiel's prophecies indicate that Turkey will be one of the ten nations. In Ezekiel 38 and 39 we are told about "the chief prince" of several ancient territories which today are part of Turkey. The "chief prince" is the Antichrist and he rule over the ten nations which will include Turkey. The nations of the Antichrist will ultimately gather and come against Jerusalem at the time of the Messiah's return, on the "Day of the Lord."

Below is a Hebrew map of the ancient territories mentioned in
Ezekiel chapter thirty eight.

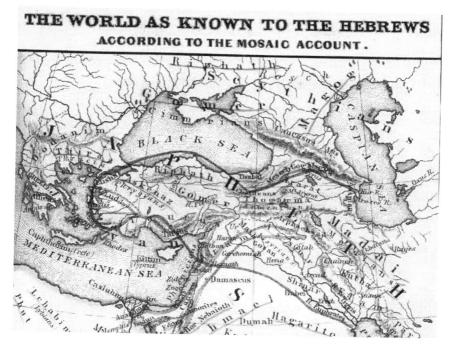

THE WORLD AS KNOWN TO THE HEBREWS
ACCORDING TO THE MOSAIC ACCOUNT.

Therefore, Turkey will join with the other nine nations to form the
Fourth Beast Kingdom of the Antichrist.

So far we have identified five of the ten nations that will comprise
the Fourth Beast Kingdom of the Antichrist.

1. Iraq
2. Egypt
3. Libya
4. Sudan, Northern
5. Turkey

At this point, let's look a couple of common factors regarding the ten nations of the Antichrist. First, is that they all are related to the Statue prophecy of Daniel chapter two. Daniel two gives us the historical kingdom perspective from **the head - ancient Babylon**, to **the ten toes – the final kingdom**.

Note: There are only four kingdoms mentioned in the statue prophecy and the first three are historical; Babylon, Media-Persia and Greece. This leaves only the Fourth and final kingdom of the Antichrist which Daniel also described in chapters 7, 8, 9 and 11. Also, note that Rome is not mentioned.

When we take a look at the geographical area historically encompassed by the enormous, dazzling statue of Daniel, we see more than ten nations.

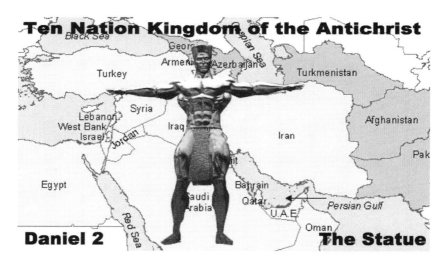

There will only be ten nations that join together to form the future kingdom of the Antichrist. Therefore, we must search the Scripture to see, what else will bind these ten nations together?

Besides geography what else do the prophets tells us about the ten that will enable us to find the other five?

They All Hate the USA

The prophet John was told about the identity of Mystery Babylon the Great and the Beast Kingdom on which she rides in Revelation 17. Here is how that is written.

> "I will explain to you the mystery of the woman [Babylon the Great] and of the beast [Antichrist] she rides, which has the seven heads and ten horns" (Revelation 17:7).

As we read the Revelation 17 prophecy we should keep in mind that to "sit on" or to "ride" something signifies a position of dominance. Therefore, Mystery Babylon initially is dominant over the Middle Eastern Kingdom of the Antichrist. Therefore, the USA will keep her position of dominance until the Antichrist and his ten nation kingdom comes against the USA as we read below.

> "The beast [Antichrist] and the ten horns you saw **will hate** the prostitute (USA). **They will** bring her to ruin and leave her naked; they will eat her flesh and **burn her with fire**" (Revelation 17:16).

Just as we have seen, previously, the Antichrist and all ten kings will hate Babylon the Great and bring her to ruin by burning her with fire. So, who are the other five nations who hate the USA? Today, the US is becoming less and less popular in the Middle East. However, after we see the violence and destruction caused by the leader of the Babylonians in Habakkuk 2, many more nations will come to hate the USA.

If I were to make a guess today, I would add the follow five nations to our list; Syria, Lebanon, Iran, Afghanistan and Pakistan. So if I am correct the list of the ten nations will look something like this:

1. Iraq
2. Egypt
3. Libya
4. Sudan
5. Turkey
6. Syria
7. Lebanon
8. Iran
9. Afghanistan
10. Pakistan

Reviewing the information we have covered in this chapter, we have learned the following about the time of the Fourth Seal prophecy:

- Egypt is symbolized by the Pale Horse.
- This war starts with Egypt engaging the Antichrist.
- The Antichrist is victorious.
- Antichrist confirms a covenant with Israel.
- Egypt, Libya and Sudan in submission to Antichrist.

Chapter 9
Seven Trumpets

We have examined and discussed the horses and riders of the first four seals of Revelation. The first four seals have taken us through years of wars, famines, pestilences and earthquakes and delivered us to the last seven years of the Time of the End. Daniel wrote about the Antichrist and the last seven years below,

> "He [Antichrist] will confirm a covenant with many for one 'seven.' In the middle of the 'seven' he will put an end to sacrifice and offering. And on a wing of the temple he will set up an abomination that causes desolation, until the end that is decreed is poured out on him" (Daniel 9:27).

After the Antichrist's Fourth Seal victory, when he subdues Egypt, Libya and Sudan, there will be peace and security for Israel for 3.5 years. Paul wrote about this tenuous time of peace and safety that would precede the Great Tribulation.

> "While people are saying, "Peace and safety," destruction will come on them suddenly, as labor pains on a pregnant woman, and they will not escape" (1 Thessalonians 5:3).

Great Tribulation Begins

After the 3.5 years of peace and safety, in the middle of the seven, the Antichrist will return to Jerusalem and set himself up in Yahweh's Temple and declare that he is God. This event is called the "abomination that causes desolation" and it precedes the Second Coming by about 3.5 years. The apostle Paul described the "abomination that causes desolation" below.

> "Concerning the coming of our Lord Jesus Christ and our being gathered to him, … that day will not come until … the man of lawlessness is revealed, the man doomed to destruction. He will oppose and will exalt himself over everything that is called God or is worshiped, so that he sets himself up in God's temple, proclaiming himself to be God" (2 Thessalonians 2:1-4).

The Messiah also warned us about this time when the Antichrist would stand in the Temple. He warned us to be ready to flee Judea in haste because this would be the time of Great Tribulation. Christ described this time of Great Tribulation much the same way Daniel had written. Compare their two prophecies below.

> "At that time Michael, the great prince who protects your people, will arise. **There will be a time of distress such as has not happened from the beginning of nations until then**. But at that time your people--everyone whose name is found written in the book--will be delivered" (Daniel 12:1).

> Messiah: "For then **there will be great tribulation, unequaled from the beginning of the world until now**--and never to be equaled again" (Matthew 24:21).

Duration of the Tribulation

The Great Tribulation will last 3.5 biblical years. A biblical year consists of twelve 30 day months or 360 days. Prophecy records the duration of the Great Tribulation eight times, as listed below:

1. Time, times and half a time – Daniel 7:25
2. In the middle of the seven – Daniel 9:27

3. Time, times and half a time – Daniel 12:7
4. 42 months – Revelation 11:2
5. 1,260 days – Revelation 11:3
6. 1,260 days - Revelation 12:6
7. Time, times and half a time – Revelation 12:14
8. 42 months – Revelation 13:5

Each of these references are used to describe different things that will be happening during that 3.5 year Great Tribulation. Understanding this will help us solve several prophetic mysteries.

For example:

John saw Satan fall from heaven

One of these mysteries is regarding when Satan's thrown down from heaven to earth. Some people have gotten the impression, from one of Christ's statements that Satan has already been cast down from heaven. Christ said,

> "I saw Satan fall like lightning from heaven" (Luke 10:18).

However, the question remains, when did Christ see Satan fall? Did Christ see this at some time in the past or was Christ speaking prophetically about a future event? Once again the Bible will answer our question.

We see in Revelation 12 that Satan will be thrown down from heaven to earth at a certain moment in the Time of the End. Let's look at what John wrote about this vision. I should also point out that John, like Christ, also saw Satan fall from heaven. Yet that event has not yet happened. Therefore, we can see what Christ meant when we compare it to what John wrote.

"There was war in heaven. **Michael** [Archangel] and his angels fought against the dragon, and the dragon and his angels fought back. But he was not strong enough, and they lost their place in heaven. The great dragon was hurled down--that ancient serpent called the devil, or **Satan**, who leads the whole world astray. **He was hurled to the earth, and his angels with him**" (Revelation 12:7-9).

Here we have a clear description of the event when Satan and his angels lose their place in heaven and are hurled down to the earth. We are told that the Archangel Michael is the one who started this war with Satan. Therefore, the appointed time came and God ordered Michael to throw the bum out. But when did this happen? This happens 3.5 years before the end of the age. This happens in the middle of the last seven years. This happens at the very time of the "abomination that causes desolation", when the Antichrist goes into the Temple of Yahweh and proclaims that he is God. John wrote,

> **"When the dragon [Satan] saw that he had been hurled to the earth**, he pursued the woman [Israel] who had given birth to the male child. The woman was given the two wings of a great eagle, so that she might fly to the place prepared for her in the desert, where she would be taken care of **for a time, times and half a time**, out of the serpent's reach" (Revelation 12;13-14).

When we realize a couple of other things from Scripture we may be able to solve another of the Bible's prophetic mysteries.

First, Michael the Archangel is assigned to protect God's people as we read below in Daniel's prophecies.

> "At that time **Michael, the great prince who protects your people**, will arise. There will be a time of distress such as has not happened from the beginning of nations until then" (Daniel 12:1).

"But I will show thee that which is noted in the scripture of truth: and there is **none that holdeth with me in these things, but Michael** your prince" (KJV Daniel 10:21)

All Hell Breaks Loose

Reviewing what we know so far, Michael the protector of God's people throws Satan and his angels to earth at the time the "Great Tribulation" begins. The Great Tribulation is to be a time of unprecedented persecution and death for Yahweh's people. Christ said,

> "For then there will be **Great Tribulation**, unequaled from the beginning of the world until now--and never to be equaled again. If those days had not been cut short, no one would survive" (Matthew 24:21).

Michael, the protector of God's people, the great prince who holds back Satan, hurls Satan to earth. Michael does this at the very time that the Antichrist is in the Temple proclaiming that he is God. Then Antichrist begins to persecute God's people and the Great Tribulation begins.

Below is how Paul explained this about Michael and Satan at the time that the Antichrist is revealed.

> "And now you know what is holding him back, so that he [Antichrist] may be revealed at the proper time. For the secret power of lawlessness [Satan] is already at work; but the one who now holds it back will continue to do so till he [Michael] is taken out of the way. And then the lawless one [Antichrist] will be revealed, whom the Lord Jesus will overthrow with the breath of his mouth and destroy by the splendor of his coming. The coming of the lawless one [Antichrist] will be in accordance with the work of Satan displayed in all kinds of counterfeit miracles, signs and wonders" (2 Thessalonians 2:6-9).

As soon as Satan is no longer being restrained by Michael, the Antichrist is revealed by proclaiming that he is God in Yahweh's Temple.

Now that we see that it is Michael who is currently holding back Satan we can begin to understand the magnitude of what will happen next. As we just read above, the coming of the Antichrist will be displayed with all kinds of counterfeit miracles, signs and wonders. In other words when Satan is cut loose some amazing things are going to happen, supernatural things.

Christ warned us that this would happen during the Great Tribulation when He said,

> "For false Christs and false prophets will appear and perform great signs and miracles to deceive even the elect--if that were possible. See, I have told you ahead of time' (Matthew 24:24-25).

When the Great Tribulation begins we can expect to see the level of spiritual warfare escalate dramatically. Things will begin to happen that can only be explained in prophecy. That is another reason we must know Scripture. I believe it is imperative that all Yahweh's people read and understand Scripture. We must know what Scripture says in order that we are not deceived by false prophets and their counterfeit miracles, signs and wonders.

We will now begin to examine the Seven Trumpets of Revelation. I believe that the trumpets of Revelation will serve as warning signs for Yahweh's people as they go through the Great Tribulation. That's right there will be no Pre-Tribulation Rapture for Yahweh's people. Yahweh's people all of them, both Hebrew and Gentile, who are alive and left must go through the Great Tribulation.

Let's go back to the seal prophecies for a moment. It's likely that the Fifth Seal prophecy marks the beginning of the Antichrist's persecution of Yahweh's people at the Great Tribulation. Since each of the seals so far have been about wars in the Time of the End, it's possible that the Fifth Seal marks Antichrist's War on the People of Yahweh, His Saints.

The Fifth Seal appears to be opened at the time that the Great Tribulation begins. This would also be the time when the Trumpet warnings begin to sound during the last 3.5 years of Antichrist's persecution of the Saints. Here is what the 5th Seal and the trumpets would look like on our timeline.

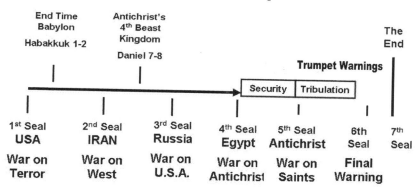

I will discuss the 6th Seal later in regard to the Second Coming.

Back to the Trumpet Warnings:

First Trumpets

There are several reasons why I believe the trumpets of Revelation span the Great Tribulation.

First, as the first trumpets are sounded something is being thrown down upon the earth. This corresponds well to what we have been discussing about Satan and his angels. Satan and his angels will be thrown down upon the earth at the time of the Great Tribulation which will likely be at the same time that the trumpets are being sounded.

> "**The first** angel sounded his trumpet, and there came hail and fire mixed with blood, and it was **hurled down upon the earth**. A third of the earth was burned up, a third of the trees were burned up, and all the green grass was burned up. **The second** angel sounded his trumpet, and something like a huge mountain, all ablaze, was **thrown into the sea**. A third of the sea turned into blood, a third of the living creatures in the sea died, and a third of the ships were destroyed. **The third** angel sounded his trumpet, and a great star, blazing like a torch, **fell from the sky** on a third of the rivers and on the springs of water-- the name of the star is Wormwood. A third of the waters turned bitter, and many people died from the waters that had become bitter" (Revelation 8:7-11).

I do not, at this time, have any special insight or revelation concerning these first three prophecies other than – they mean what they say.

Before we continue I will mention the second reason I believe the trumpet warnings span the Time of the End. The 7th and last trumpet of revelation will signal the return of the Messiah to begin His reign on earth as we read below.

> "The seventh angel sounded his trumpet, and there were loud voices in heaven, which said: "The kingdom of the world has become the kingdom of our Lord and of his Christ, and he will reign for ever and ever" (Revelation 11:15).

We will be discussing the Second Coming of Christ at the 7th trumpet in detail, after we examine the remaining trumpet warnings.

Next is the Fourth Trumpet warning and the earth begins to get dark.

"**The fourth** angel sounded his trumpet, and a third of the sun was struck, a third of the moon, and a third of the stars, so that a third of them turned dark. A third of the day was without light, and also a third of the night" (Revelation 8:12).

When the fifth trumpet warning sounds, it appears that Satan, who has been thrown down, will open the abyss and release demons to torment all those who are not Yahweh's people. Here is why I believe that this star is none other than Satan himself.

"How you have fallen from heaven, O **morning star, son of the dawn! You have been cast down to the earth**, you who once laid low the nations! You said in your heart, "I will ascend to heaven; I will raise my throne above the stars of God; I will sit enthroned on the mount of assembly, on the utmost heights of the sacred mountain" (Isaiah 14:12-13).

Here is why I believe these creatures in the abyss are demons.

"Jesus asked him, 'What is your name?' 'Legion,' he replied, because many demons had gone into him. And they begged him repeatedly not to order them to go into the Abyss" (Luke 8:30-31).

Satan opens the Abyss

Now, let's see how John describes this amazing scene when Satan opens the abyss and releases all these demons to torment the people of the world.

"**The fifth** angel sounded his trumpet, and I saw **a star that had fallen from the sky to the earth**. The star was given the key to the shaft of the Abyss. When he opened the Abyss, smoke rose from it like the smoke from a gigantic furnace. The sun and sky were darkened by the smoke from the Abyss. And out of the smoke locusts came down upon the earth and were given power like that of scorpions of the earth. They were told not to harm the grass of the earth or any plant or tree, but only those people who did not have the seal of God on their foreheads. They were not given power to kill them, but only to torture them for five months. And the agony they suffered was like that of the sting of a scorpion when it strikes a man. During those days men will seek death, but will not find it; they will long to die, but death will elude them" (Revelation 9:1-6).

In verses seven through nine, John describes the demons. I have left out their description because like many of the supernatural things in many of John's visions, we who are alive and left at that time, will not likely see these supernatural creatures. We will, however, recognize the fulfillment of the prophecy by what is happening to those who are not Yahweh's people.

Finally, John identifies the leader of these demons by using his Greek and Hebrew names. The king of the Abyss is none other than the Destroyer who we may remember from the time of Passover and the Exodus from ancient Egypt. If you don't remember you can find him in Exodus 12:23.

"They had as king over them the angel of the Abyss, whose name in Hebrew is Abaddon, and in Greek, Apollyon." (Revelation 9:11).

We have seen some amazing things in John's visions up to this point. We are seeing things which will occur late in the Great Tribulation. The world has already been through horrendous war after horrendous war. The world is experiencing things that are inexplicable, yet Yahweh's people will realize what is happening because they were told about them in Bible prophecy ahead of time.

Never the less, the world continues head-long on its path toward Judgment Day with little or no thought of repentance. What we will see next in John's vision of the trumpets will set the stage for that final conflict. The nations of the earth will gather for the final battle against the Messiah the King, on the Day of the Lord.

Let's look at the sixth trumpet.

> **"The sixth** angel sounded his **trumpet** ... Release the four angels who are bound at the great river Euphrates. And the four angels who had been kept ready for this very hour and day and month and year were released **to kill a third of mankind.** The number of the mounted troops was two hundred million. I heard their number. The horses and riders I saw in my vision looked like this: Their breastplates were fiery red, dark blue, and yellow as sulfur. The heads of the horses resembled the heads of lions, and out of their mouths came fire, smoke and sulfur. **A third of mankind was killed** by the three plagues of fire, smoke and sulfur that came out of their mouths. The power of the horses was in their mouths and in their tails; for their tails were like snakes, having heads with which they inflict injury. The rest of mankind that were not killed by these plagues **still did not repent"** (Revelation 9:13-20).

When John saw these visions he was in the spirit and he saw things both supernatural and natural that would take place during the Time of the End and during the Great Tribulation. As we see in the vision above, it is currently impossible to understand which of these things are supernatural and which are natural. I do not believe that these things are written so we can make that determination now. I believe that Yahweh has made these visions known so that when His people reach this part of the Great Tribulation, they will be able to know what is happening just as they know Who it is that warned them about these things ahead of time.

At this point in John's visions, just before the seventh trumpet, we are close to the Messiah's return. Before we look at the seventh trumpet we should understand some things about the Feasts of Yahweh and their significance to the coming of the Messiah. The reason we are discussing this now is because the Seventh Trumpet will mark the prophetic fulfillment of Yahweh's Feast of Trumpets.

The Feast of Yahweh

The Feast of Trumpets is the next feast that will be fulfilled by the Messiah. It is the fifth of seven and the first feast day of Yahweh's Fall Harvest Festival of Ingathering. The Fall Harvest Festival of Ingathering includes the final three Feasts of Yahweh; the Day of Trumpets, the Day of Atonement and the greatest of all the feasts, the seven day Feast of Tabernacles. The Feast of Tabernacles is also known in the New Testament as the Wedding Banquet.

Did you know that all the seven Feasts of Yahweh point to the Messiah? The Feasts of Yahweh help Yahweh's people understand what the Messiah has done for them as well as what He is going to do.

The early Feasts of Yahweh where filled by the Messiah at the time of His First Coming. The final Fall Feasts of Yahweh will be fulfilled by the Messiah at His Second Coming. Since the First Coming is history, let's see how the Messiah fulfilled the first four Feasts of Yahweh at that time.

The Feast of Passover is perhaps the easiest to see. It is relatively well known that the Messiah, call Christ, is the Passover Lamb as we see recorded below.

> "For **Christ, our Passover lamb**, has been sacrificed. Therefore **let us keep the Festival,** not with the old yeast, the yeast of malice and wickedness, but with bread without yeast, the bread of sincerity and truth" (1 Corinthians 5:7-8).

Perhaps, if the Church had been keeping the Festivals as the apostle Paul instructed, the feasts would not be as unknown as they are today. Paul said this about keeping the Passover Festival.

> "For Christ, our Passover lamb, has been sacrificed. Therefore let us keep the Festival" (1 Corinthians 5:7-8).

Messiah also fulfilled the Feast of Unleavened Bread which immediately follows the day of Passover. Christ was the Unleavened Bread, the Bread without sin that came down from heaven.

> "For the bread of God is he who comes down from heaven and gives life to the world." ... Then Jesus declared, "I am the bread of life" (John 6:33, 35).

Christ is also the First Fruits the third Feast of Yahweh and He fulfilled the fourth feast at Pentecost which is the Feast of Weeks. The Feast of Weeks came seven weeks after the Day of First Fruits. Therefore, Christ is the First Fruits of Yahweh as we see below:

> "Christ has indeed been raised from the dead, the firstfruits of those who have fallen asleep. ... For as in Adam all die, so in Christ all will be made alive. ... **Christ, the firstfruits**; then, **when he comes [again]**, those who belong to him" (1 Corinthians 15:20-23).

Also, at the time of Christ's First Coming, He fulfilled the Feast of Pentecost. Pentecost is also called the Feast of Weeks because it comes seven weeks after the day of First Fruits. This feast is an earlier harvest feast and has to do with Christ providing the Holy Spirit to His people. Here is what happened when Christ fulfilled the Day of Pentecost also known as the Feast of Weeks.

"**When the day of Pentecost came**, they were all together in one place. Suddenly a sound like the blowing of a violent wind came from heaven and filled the whole house where they were sitting. They saw what seemed to be tongues of fire that separated and came to rest on each of them. **All of them were filled with the Holy Spirit** and began to speak in other tongues as the Spirit enabled them" (Acts 2:1-4).

Just as the earlier Feasts of Yahweh; Passover, Unleavened Bread, First Fruits and Pentecost were fulfilled by Christ at His First Coming, so the final Feasts of Yahweh will be fulfilled "**when he comes**" again.

The Feast of Trumpets

Since we just read above in 1 Corinthians 15 about the resurrection, let's read some more. The whole chapter of 1 Corinthians 15 is about the resurrection and I recommend it to you. In Paul's discourse on the resurrection he points us to the Feast of Trumpets as the time when all of Yahweh's people will be changed from their mortal bodies to immortal bodies. Paul makes it clear that at the last trumpet all God's people, those who have died and those still alive and left, will be resurrected. Here is how Paul wrote this;

"**Listen, I tell you a mystery**: We will not all sleep, but **we will all be changed**-- in a flash, in the twinkling of an eye, **at the last trumpet**. For the trumpet will sound, the dead will be raised imperishable, and we will be changed. For the perishable must clothe itself with the imperishable, and the mortal with immortality" (1 Corinthians 15:51-53).

Now, let's pick up where we left off back in Revelation. The sixth trumpet had sounded and heaven and earth are getting ready for the final battle on the Day of Yahweh (the LORD). Following from **the mystery** that the prophet Paul was telling us about above, let's pick up in Revelation when the seventh and last trumpet is about to be sounded. Here is what John wrote as the seventh trumpet is about to be sounded,

"But in the days **when the seventh** angel is about to sound his trumpet, **the mystery** of God will be accomplished, just as he announced to his servants the prophets" (Revelation 10:7).

Wow! Paul tells us about a resurrection mystery that will be accomplished at the Last Trumpet. Now, John tells us the same thing! **The mystery will be accomplished at the seventh and last trumpet.** So what happens when the Seventh Trumpet is sounded?

"**The seventh** angel sounded his trumpet, and there were loud voices in heaven, which said: '**The kingdom of the world has become the kingdom of our Lord and of his Christ,** and he will reign for ever and ever'" (Revelation 11:15).

At the last trumpet, Christ is back and He is ruler of the world, the Kingdom of God has finally come. So, if Christ returns and establishes His kingdom on earth at the seventh and last trumpet, how does this fit with Christ fulfilling all the Feasts of Yahweh?

The Feast of Trumpets is the opening feast of the Fall Festival called the Festival of Ingathering. The first six trumpets of Revelation warn Yahweh's people that the Day of Trumpets is approaching. In Israel trumpets are sounded each day as the Feast of Trumpets approaches.

When the Day of Trumpets arrives at the New Moon of the seventh month, all the trumpets signal that the Festival of Ingathering has begun. This is the first day of the seventh month. It begins on "the day and hour" when two witness first see the sign of the New Moon crescent. Sometimes due to the weather, the new crescent is not visible. That's why the Israelites sometimes call this New Moon Feast of Trumpets, "the feast which no one knows the day or hour." Sounds like something Christ once said,

"No one knows about that day or hour, not even the angels in heaven, nor the Son, but only the Father" (Mark 13:32).

Perhaps it's a clue regarding His Second Coming on the Day of Trumpets?

The next feast after the Day of Trumpets is the Day of Atonement. The Day of Trumpets takes place on the first day of the seventh month and the Day of Atonement takes place on the tenth day. The Day of Atonement is when Yahweh's people are to deny themselves. It's most likely judgment day for God's people, when they will be rewarded for their work. In the New Testament writings it's called the Judgment seat of Christ.

> "For we must all appear before the judgment seat of Christ, that each one may receive what is due him for the things done while in the body, whether good or bad" (2 Corinthians 5:10).

We also see that Christ will judge His people following their gathering at time of the seventh trumpet in Revelation. After the resurrection gathering at the last trumpet, Christ will judge His people as John recorded.

> "The time has come **for judging** the dead, and **for rewarding** your servants the prophets and **your saints** and those who reverence your name, both small and great" (Revelation 11:18).

This takes us through the John's Seventh Trumpet prophecies which clearly ties to the Feasts of Yahweh and the Second Coming of the Messiah.

Sixth Seal Prophecy

In the next chapter we will be discussing in detail what Scripture has to say about the Second Coming of the Messiah, called Christ. But before we do, we need to examine and discuss the Sixth Seal prophecy. The Sixth Seal prophecy will reveal some very important things about the timing of the Second Coming, some things you may not have heard before.

First, let's get a visual perspective from our timeline.

Time of the End: 6ᵗʰ Seal

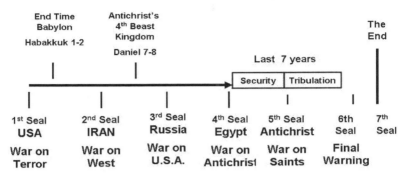

The timeline indicates that the 6ᵗʰ Seal is opened after the Great Tribulation, but before the Second Coming. How do we know that is true? Once again, we know what is true, not based on what we have heard from Man, but from the Word of Yahweh. We will again turn to Scripture to determine when the Sixth Seal is opened. Here is the Sixth Seal prophecy.

> "I watched as he opened **the sixth seal**. There was a great earthquake. **The sun turned black like sackcloth made of goat hair, the whole moon turned blood red, and the stars in the sky fell to earth**, as late figs drop from a fig tree when shaken by a strong wind. The sky receded like a scroll, rolling up, and every mountain and island was removed from its place. Then the kings of the earth, the princes, the generals, the rich, the mighty, and every slave and every free **man hid in caves and among the rocks of the mountains**. They called to the mountains and the rocks, "Fall on us and hide us from the face of him who sits on the throne and from the wrath of the Lamb! **For the great day of their wrath has come**, and who can stand?" (Revelation 6:12-17).

What we see here is that the Sixth Seal opens when "**The sun turned black like sackcloth made of goat hair, the whole moon turned blood red, and the stars in the sky fell to earth**." When does Scripture say these things will happen? Christ said these things would happen immediately after the Great Tribulation.

> "Immediately <u>after the tribulation</u> of those days '**the sun will be darkened, and the moon will not give its light; the stars will fall from the sky**'" (Matthew 24:29).

The prophet Joel said these things would happen before the Day of Yahweh (the LORD). Here Joel describes these signs in the sun, moon and stars as taking place before Yahweh (the LORD) returns with His army.

> "**Before them** the earth shakes, **the sky trembles, the sun and moon are darkened, and the stars no longer shine**. The LORD thunders at the head of his army; his forces are beyond number, and mighty are those who obey his command. The day of the LORD is great; it is dreadful. Who can endure it?" Joel 2:10-11).

Similarly, Joel describes these signs in the heavens and on earth as occurring before the Day of Yahweh (the LORD.

> "I will show wonders in the heavens and on the earth, blood and fire and billows of smoke. **The sun will be turned to darkness and the moon to blood <u>before</u>** the coming of **the great and dreadful day of the LORD**" (Joel 2:30-31).

This sign in the sun, moon and stars is mentioned by several of the prophets, including Isaiah and Ezekiel, in connection to the coming Day of Yahweh. From the passages we just read from Matthew and Joel we are able to determine that the Six Seal will be opened just before the Second Coming of the Messiah – after the Tribulation and before the Day of the LORD.

Just as we see in our 6th Seal timeline.

Time of the End: 6th Seal

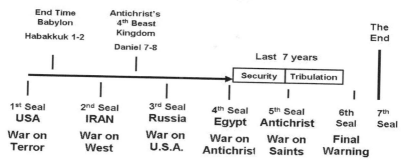

There is much more that happens after the Messiah's return which we will discuss next in Chapter 10, The Second Coming.

What we now know:

- When the Great Tribulation Starts
- When the Fifth Seal opens.
- About Supernatural and Natural Trumpet Warnings
- When the Sixth Seal opens.
- About the Seventh and Last Trumpet
- When the Kingdom Comes.

Chapter 10
The Second Coming

In this chapter we will be carefully examining the Second Coming of the Messiah, called Christ. The coming of the Messiah as King of the world has been a central aspect of the gospel from the beginning in Genesis. Most of Yahweh's prophets have written about the coming Day of the LORD and Kingdom of God on earth. From the prophets various accounts, we are able to visualize one of the most dramatic scenes ever described in the Bible – Christ's physical, visual reappearing. When the Second Coming happens it will End "this age" and begin to usher in the "age to come." When the Messiah returns He will begin to reign for thousand years in the eternal Kingdom of God on earth.

So far we have been discussing the seven seals and the seven trumpets of Revelation. As we have seen the seven seals will span the "Time of the End" from the First Seal and the West's War on Terror to the Seventh Seal and the opening of the Book of Life.

When the Seventh Seal is removed, the Scroll of Life will be opened and the angels will know who Yahweh's people are. The angels will be ready and able to gather them to the Lord in air. Here is how the Seventh Seal appears on our timeline.

Time of the End: 7th Seal

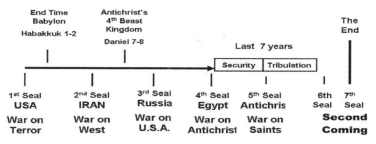

The seven trumpets will span the "Great Tribulation" from the time Satan is thrown down from heaven to earth to the Seventh Trumpet when the world becomes Christ's kingdom.

Let's begin our examination of the Second Coming with Christ's account as recorded in Matthew 24. Matthew 24 and 25 record His response to the disciples when they asked Him what would be a sign that the Time of the End had come for His return. His response to them described several signs that would take place leading up to His return at the end of the age. Then Christ described in detail the event of His Second Coming.

First, let me tell you what He told His disciples. Then I will show you what Christ told His disciples. Here are the details:

Christ's Appearing

1) His coming will be after the Great Tribulation.
2) After the Tribulation will be a sign in the sun, moon and stars.
3) The sun, moon and stars sign precedes the Day of the LORD.
4) Christ comes and appears in the sky on the Day of the LORD.
5) When the trumpet sounds all Yahweh's people will be instantly resurrected (changed from mortal to immortal).
6) Then the angels will gather His people to the Messiah; those who have died - from heaven and those who are still alive - from earth.

Now, here is what Christ said:

> "Immediately **after the tribulation** of those days 'the sun will be darkened, and the moon will not give its light; the stars will fall from the sky, and the heavenly bodies will be shaken.' At that time the sign of the Son of Man will appear in the sky, and all the nations of the earth will mourn. They will **see the Son of Man coming** on the clouds of the sky, with power and great glory. And he will send his angels with a loud **trumpet call**, and **they will gather his elect** from the four winds, from one end of the heavens to the other" (Matthew 24:29-31).

Since this describes Christ's Second Coming to earth, He must have come down from heaven when He appears in the clouds of the sky. This idea is supported by Paul's description of Christ's return. Below is how Paul described the Second Coming.

> "Jesus died and rose again and so we believe that **God will bring with Jesus those who have fallen asleep** in him. According to the Lord's own word, we tell you that we who are still alive, who are left till the coming of the Lord, will certainly not precede those who have fallen asleep. For **the Lord himself will come down from heaven**, with a loud command, with the voice of the archangel and with **the trumpet** call of God, and the dead in Christ will rise first. After that, **we who are still alive and are left will be caught up together with them in the clouds to meet the Lord in the air**" (1 Thessalonians 4:14-17).

Unlike the Matthew 24 account, Paul's account does not specifically say that this event takes place after the Great Tribulation. However, Paul says, "the Lord himself will come down from heaven" which like Matthew 24 indicates that the Second Coming is after the Tribulation. How do we know that?

At the Appointed Time

The Bible is clear that Christ **must** stay in heaven **until** the appointed time for His return. Here are two prophecies that confirm that His Second Coming will be when Christ establishes His Kingdom on earth and defeats His enemies.

> "**He must remain in heaven until** the time comes for God to restore everything, as he promised long ago through his holy prophets" (Acts 3:21).

Since we know that God does not restore everything until His Kingdom Comes – the Second Coming will be after the Tribulation. And since we also know that Christ's enemies are not defeated until after the Tribulation this next verse confirms the same timing.

> "The Lord said to my Lord: '**Sit at my right hand until** I make your enemies a footstool for your feet'" (Acts 2:34).

Since, Christ cannot leave heaven until the appointed time, each of these "Second Coming" accounts indicate a return after the Great Tribulation.

When Christ leaves heaven, comes down into the clouds of the sky and gathers His people; heaven will be above and the earth below as we see in this description found in the Psalms.

> "**Our God comes** and will not be silent; a fire devours before him, and around him a tempest rages. He summons **the heavens above, and the earth,** that he may judge his people: '**Gather to me my consecrated ones**, who made a covenant with me by sacrifice'" (Psalm 50:3-5).

After Christ has left heaven, come down into the clouds of the sky and gathered up His followers, where does He go from there? As usual Scripture has the answer.

Return to the Mount of Olives

Again, we find the answer in Acts.

"Men of Galilee," they said, "why do you stand here looking into the sky? **This same Jesus**, who has been taken from you into heaven, **will come back in the same way you have seen him go into heaven**." Then they returned to Jerusalem from the hill called the Mount of Olives" (Acts 1:11-12).

According to this passage, Jesus will return the same way He left earth for heaven. Therefore, once Christ has gathered up His people in the clouds of the sky He will descend to the Mount of Olives, the same place from which he ascended. This description is also supported by the following Second Coming prophecy which indicates that on the Day of the Lord Christ will stand on the Mount of Olives.

> "**On that day his feet will stand on the Mount of Olives**, east of Jerusalem, and the Mount of Olives will be split in two from east to west, forming a great valley, with half of the mountain moving north and half moving south. ... Then **the LORD my God will come, and all the holy ones with him**" (Zechariah 14:4-5).

We should also keep in mind that we are with Him when He descends to the Mount of Olives. We know this from the passage above and Paul's first letter to the Thessalonians when He said, "After that, we who are still alive and are left will be caught up together with them in the clouds to meet the Lord in the air. **And so we will be with the Lord forever**" (1 Thessalonians 4:17).

From the Mount of Olives, where do we go?

Return to the Temple Mount

The prophet Micah indicates that after the LORD has gather up His people he will pass from the Mount of Olives and return to the Temple Mount through the Eastern Gate.

"I will surely gather all of you, O Jacob; I will surely bring together the remnant of Israel. I will bring them together like sheep in a pen, like a flock in its pasture; the place will throng with people. One who breaks open the way will go up before them; they will break **through the gate** and go out. **Their king will pass through before them, the LORD at their head**" (Micah 2:12-13).

"Then suddenly **the Lord you are seeking will come to his temple**; the messenger of the covenant, whom you desire, will come," says the LORD Almighty. But who can endure the day of his coming? Who can stand **when he appears**? For he will be like a refiner's fire or a launderer's soap" (Malachi 3:1-2).

There are several accounts of the Lord's coming recoded in the prophets which present a spectacular picture of the Second Coming. Let's take a look and see how the prophets describe this Big Screen event. Remember that the sun, moon and stars have gone dark just before His return, making His glorious appearing in the sky like lightening that much more spectacular.

Every eye will see.

Let's take a look at several of the prophecies about the Second Coming to see just how spectacular the Messiah's return will be. I will bold things from each account that I find particularly interesting. After each account I will mention an item of the prophecy that I believe contributes to our understanding about Christ's return.

"Look, he is coming with the clouds, and **every eye will see him, even those who pierced him;** and all the peoples of the earth will mourn because of him. So shall it be! Amen" (Revelation 1:7).

No one will miss the Messiah's Second Coming, no one!

"In my distress I called to the LORD; I called out to my God. From his temple he heard my voice; my cry came to his ears. The earth trembled and quaked, the foundations of the heavens shook; they trembled because he was angry. Smoke rose from his nostrils; consuming fire came from his mouth, burning coals blazed out of it. **He parted the heavens and came down; dark clouds were under his feet**. He mounted the cherubim and flew; he soared on the wings of the wind. He made darkness his canopy around him-- the dark rain clouds of the sky. Out of the brightness of his presence bolts of lightning blazed Fourth. **The LORD thundered from heaven**; the voice of the Most High resounded. He shot arrows and scattered the enemies, bolts of lightning and routed them. The valleys of the sea were exposed and the foundations of the earth laid bare at the rebuke of the LORD, at the blast of breath from his nostrils. **He reached down from on high and took hold of me**; he drew me out of deep waters. He rescued me from my powerful enemy, from my foes, who were too strong for me. They confronted me in the day of my disaster, but the LORD was my support. **He brought me out into a spacious place**" (2 Samuel 22:7-20).

We can clearly see that the LORD is in the clouds of the sky when He returns and gathers up those of His followers who are still alive and left. This agrees exactly with what Christ said and Paul wrote in the New Testament accounts.

The Rapture

As many of you may know this "catching up" event is often referred to in modern church theology as the "Rapture." Here it is described as, "He reached down from on high and took hold of me" and "He brought me out into a spacious place." The second part, "He brought me out into a spacious place" is a perfect description of what it will be like to be in the clouds of the sky above the earth when we are gathered to be with the LORD.

Several Old Testament prophets reveal common details of the LORD's appearing as well as other things that will be happening at the time of His coming. Their accounts will help us fill in details of that time. Here are a couple examples:

> "Oh, that **you would rend the heavens and come down, that the mountains would tremble before you!** As when fire sets twigs ablaze and causes water to boil, come down to make your name known to your enemies and **cause the nations to quake** before you! For when you did awesome things that we did not expect, you came down, and the mountains trembled before you. Since ancient times no one has heard, no ear has perceived, no eye has seen any God besides **you, who acts on behalf of those who wait for him. You come to the help of those who gladly do right, <u>who remember your ways</u>**" (Isaiah 64:1-5).

The Lord comes to help those who are waiting for Him, those who have not forgotten nor failed to be obedient to God's ways.

> "Look! The LORD is coming from his dwelling place; he comes down and treads the high places of the earth. **The mountains melt beneath him and the valleys split apart, like wax before the fire, like water rushing down a slope**. (Micah 1:3-4).

> "Part your heavens, O LORD, and come down; **touch the mountains, so that they smoke**. Send Fourth lightning and scatter the enemies; shoot your arrows and rout them" (Psalm 144:5-6).

Here we see that the Yahweh's coming is a fiery consumption of the earth. In Noah's time God destroyed the earth with water. When He returns He will consume the earth with fire as we see from Peter's writings. "But **the day of the Lord** will come like a thief. The heavens will disappear with a roar; the elements will be **destroyed by fire, and the earth and everything in it will be laid bare**" (2 Peter 3:10).

Even Hollywood with all their special effects would be hard pressed to effectively capture such an event as described by the prophets of Yahweh.

Jerusalem: Capital of the World

"Shout and be glad, O Daughter of Zion. For **I am coming, and I will live among you,"** declares the LORD. Many nations will be joined with the LORD in that day and will become my people. I will live among you and you will know that the LORD Almighty has sent me to you. **The LORD will inherit Judah as his portion in the holy land and will again choose Jerusalem**. Be still before the LORD, all mankind, because he has roused himself from his holy dwelling" (Zechariah 2:10-13).

When the LORD leaves His heavenly dwelling and comes down to the earth He will live among His people. His new residence will be Jerusalem in Judea and Israel. The Holy One of Israel will live in Jerusalem forever.

"Then **the LORD will appear over them**; his arrow will flash like lightning. The Sovereign **LORD will sound the trumpet**; he will march in the storms of the south, and the LORD Almighty will shield them. They will destroy and overcome with slingstones. They will drink and roar as with wine; they will be full like a bowl used for sprinkling the corners of the altar. **The LORD their God will save them on that day as the flock of his people**" (Zechariah 9:14-16).

Here is the Seventh and Last Trumpet we read about in 1 Corinthians 15 and Revelation 10 and 11 when God brings salvation to His people.

"See, **I will send my messenger, who will prepare the way** before me. **Then suddenly the Lord you are seeking will come to his temple**; the messenger of the covenant, whom you desire, will come," says the LORD Almighty. But who can endure the day of his coming? Who can stand when he appears? For he will be like a refiner's fire or a launderer's soap. He will sit as a refiner and purifier of silver; he will purify the Levites and refine them like gold and silver. Then the LORD will have men who will bring offerings in righteousness, and the offerings of Judah and Jerusalem will be acceptable to the LORD, as in days gone by, as in former years. **"So I will come near to you for judgment"** (Malachi 3:1-5).

A messenger will precede the Messiah's return. We are told the same thing in Revelation. John saw that there were actually two messengers who will prophesy during the 3.5 years of the Great Tribulation immediately preceding the Seventh Trumpet and the Lord's return. John wrote, "And I will give power to my two witnesses, and they will prophesy for 1,260 days (3.5 years), clothed in sackcloth" (Revelation 11:3).

Other prophecies we see in both Malachi and Revelation have to do with the judgment of Yahweh's people. Malachi wrote, "So I will come near to you for judgment." John wrote of this same judgment, "The time has come for judging the dead, and for rewarding your servants the prophets and your saints and those who reverence your name, both small and great" (Revelation 11:18).

Now, let me introduce you to another rider on a white horse. There can be absolutely no doubt about the identity of this rider because this rider is the KING OF KINGS AND LORD OF LORDS

"I saw **heaven standing open** and there before me was a white horse, whose rider is called Faithful and True. With justice he judges and makes war. His eyes are like blazing fire, and on his head are many crowns. He has a name written on him that no one knows but he himself. He is dressed in a robe dipped in blood, and his name is the Word of God. The armies of heaven were following him, riding on white horses and dressed in fine linen, white and clean. Out of his mouth comes a sharp sword with which to strike down the nations. "He will rule them with an iron scepter." **He treads the winepress of the fury of the wrath of God Almighty.** On his robe and on his thigh he has this name written: KING OF KINGS AND LORD OF LORDS. And I saw an angel standing in the sun, who cried in a loud voice to all the birds flying in midair, "Come, gather together for the great supper of God, so that you may eat the flesh of kings, generals, and mighty men, of horses and their riders, and the flesh of all people, free and slave, small and great." Then I saw **the beast and the kings of the earth and their armies gathered together to make war against the rider** on the horse and his army" (Revelation 19:11-19).

In the account of the Lord's coming we see that the kings of the earth have gathered together to make war against the Messiah. We also see that the wrath of God will be poured out at the time of His coming.

As we have read each of these prophecies about the Second Coming we have encountered many different things that will happen. It should be obvious that all these things will not happen at the same moment. Some things will happen before others. Some things may happen one moment to the next while others may take several days to transpire. Fortunately, Scripture appears to give us the information we need to understand the order of events that will take place on the Day of the LORD a.k.a. the Day of Yahweh.

Below is an ordered list the various events which we encountered in the prophecies above. We have already determined the sequence of some of these items. For the rest, I will show you from Scripture why these things will happen in this order

On the Day of the LORD

1. He comes after the Great Tribulation.
2. The sun, moon and stars sign precedes the Day of the LORD.
3. When the last trumpet sounds all Yahweh's people will be instantly resurrected - changed from mortal to immortal.
4. The angels will gather His people to the Messiah; those who have died - from heaven and those who are still alive - from earth (rapture).
5. Christ returns to the Mount of Olives and the Temple Mount.
6. Christ judges and rewards His people.
7. Christ holds the wedding banquet for His people.
8. The LORD fights against the kings of the earth and their armies.
9. The Messiah pours out His wrath on the wicked.
10. The LORD will reside in Jerusalem forever.

I believe we have already determined the order of items 1 through 5. Therefore, I will address the remaining items; 6 through 10.

In the book of Hebrews chapter 10 and here in Colossians we are told that the law is a shadow that points to Christ; "with regard to a religious festival, a New Moon celebration or a Sabbath day. These are a shadow of the things that were to come; the reality, however, is found in Christ" (Colossians 2:16-17). So, how does the law and the festivals of Yahweh point to Christ?

In chapter 9 of this book we began touching on the Feasts of Yahweh when we were discussing the connection between the Feast of Trumpets and the Seventh and Last Trumpet of 1 Corinthians 15:51 and Revelation 11:15.

After the Day of Trumpets is the Day of Atonement. The Day of Trumpets takes place on the first day of the seventh month and the Day of Atonement takes place on the tenth day. The Day of Atonement is when the Messiah will judge and reward His people for their work. In the New Testament writings it's called the "Judgment seat of Christ."

> "For we must all appear before **the judgment seat of Christ**, that each one may receive what is due him for the things done while in the body, whether good or bad" (2 Corinthians 5:10).

This judgment of God's people on the "Day of Atonement" is the judgment we see below which comes after the seventh trumpet in Revelation.

> "The time has come for judging the dead, and for rewarding your servants the prophets and your saints and those who reverence your name, both small and great" (Revelation 11:18).

We know from the Law of Yahweh that the Day of Atonement comes on the 10th day of the seventh month, nine days after the Day of Trumpets. Therefore, as Christ fulfilled the earlier feasts at His First Coming on their appointed days, He will also fulfill the Fall Harvest Feasts at His Second Coming on their appointed days. The Judgment Seat of Christ will be nine days after Christ appears on the Day of Trumpets.

Then on the 15th day of the seventh month the greatest of all the Feasts of Yahweh, the Feast of Tabernacles, sometimes called the Feast of Booths, will begin. The Feast of Tabernacles is largest of all the feasts and it lasts for seven days. It's so big that Yahweh added a Sabbath day after the seven days of feasting as a closing assembly.

You may be asking yourself, where will Christ hold this Wedding Banquet? By now, you already know what I am going to say. Let's see what Scripture tells us about where the Wedding Banquet will be held. Based on many things that Christ taught during His First Coming, we get the impression that the banquet will be on earth. Let's see what Christ said about this feast.

> "The kingdom of heaven is like a king who prepared a wedding banquet for his son…. Tell those who have been invited that I have prepared my dinner: **My oxen and fattened cattle have been butchered**, and everything is ready. Come to the wedding banquet" (Matthew 22:2-4).

Sounds like an earthly type banquet with butchered cattle. I bet they don't even have cattle in heaven. What else did Christ say about this banquet?

> **"People will come from east and west and north and south,** and will take their places at the feast in the kingdom of God" (Luke 13:29).

Once again, this wedding feast sounds like it is on earth. People will arrive from the four points of the compass to take their places at the feast in the Kingdom which has already come. It arrived with Christ at the Seventh Trumpet as is recorded in Revelation 11:15.

So the banquet's on earth. But where on earth is the banquet? Yes, the Bible tells us where on earth it will be. Isaiah has the honor of telling where we go to attend the greatest of all of Yahweh's Feasts. Remember where we last saw Christ after He descended to earth? Correct, and that is where the wedding banquet will be held, on the Temple Mount in Jerusalem. Isaiah wrote it this way,

> "The moon will be abashed, the sun ashamed; for Yahweh Almighty will reign on **Mount Zion** and in Jerusalem, and before its elders, gloriously. … **On this mountain the LORD Almighty will prepare a feast of rich food for all peoples, a banquet of aged wine-- the best of meats and the finest of wines"** (Isaiah 24:23, 25:6).

Let's review the events of Christ's return. Christ appears in the clouds of the sky, gathers His people to Him and descends to the Mount of Olives. He then goes through the Eastern Gate to the Temple Mount (Mount Zion) where He first judges all His people at the Judgment Seat of Christ. Then He prepares the Wedding banquet on Mount Zion which will last for seven days. There, you have it according to Scripture.

What about the Battle of Armageddon?

If that's your question, then you have been watching the wrong shows on the History Channel or you have been reading the wrong books. Because there will be no Battle of Armageddon.

We have come this far together. Bear with me a little longer and I will show you some very interesting prophecies about the battle on the Great Day of the Lord. The battle almost everyone thinks is the "Battle of Armageddon."

Not Armageddon!

First, we'll look at the prophecy in Revelation that trips up almost everyone.

> "Then I saw three evil spirits that looked like frogs; they came out of the mouth of the dragon, out of the mouth of the beast [Antichrist] and out of the mouth of the false prophet… **to gather them for the battle on the great day of God Almighty**…. Then **they gathered the kings together to the place that in Hebrew is called Armageddon**" (Revelation 16:13-16).

Those so called Bible teachers, who are not familiar with what the Old Testament prophets, **often misinterpret** what this prophecy says. It says that the beast and the false prophet will gather the kings together at Armageddon for the battle on the great day. It does not say where that battle will be fought. So, where will the battle on the Great Day of the Lord be? For the answer, let's consult the prophets.

"On that day [day of the LORD], when **all the nations of the earth are gathered against her**, I will make **Jerusalem** an immovable rock for all the nations. All who try to move it will injure themselves. On that day I will strike every **horse** [army] with panic and **its rider** [leader] with madness," declares the LORD. "I will keep a watchful eye over the house of Judah, but I will blind all the **horses** [armies] of the nations" (Zechariah 12:3-4).

If you remember from our study of the horses and riders of the first four Seals of Revelation, you remember that a horse is an army and the rider is the leader of the army. With that understanding you can easily see what happens after the nations have been gathered against Jerusalem.

Zechariah was not the only other prophet to see this gathering and subsequent battle at Jerusalem. Joel wrote about this as well.

"I will **gather all nations and bring them down to the Valley of Jehoshaphat**. There I will enter into judgment against them concerning my inheritance, my people Israel, for they scattered my people among the nations and divided up my land" (Joel 3:2).

At one end of the valley of Jehoshaphat to the north is Megiddo a.k.a. Armageddon and to the south is Jerusalem as we see on the map below.

Joel's prophecy continues with his description of events following the gathering of the nations at Armageddon.

"Come quickly, all you **nations from every side, and assemble there. Bring down your warriors**, O LORD! 'Let the nations be roused; let them **advance into the Valley of Jehoshaphat**, for there I will sit to judge all the nations on every side. Swing the sickle, for the harvest is ripe. Come, trample the grapes, for the winepress is full and the vats overflow-- so great is their wickedness!' Multitudes, multitudes in the valley of decision! For the day of the LORD is near in the valley of decision. The sun and moon will be darkened, and the stars no longer shine. **The LORD will roar from Zion and thunder from Jerusalem;** the earth and the sky will tremble. But the LORD will be a refuge for his people, a stronghold for the people of Israel. 'Then you will know that I, the LORD your God, dwell in Zion, my holy hill. **Jerusalem will be holy; never again will foreigners invade her**" (Joel 3:11-17).

There you have it! On the Day of the LORD, the nations will be gathered at Armageddon and brought down the Valley of Jehoshaphat to battle against Jerusalem.

Remember where we last saw the Messiah? He was at the Wedding Feast on Mount Zion in Jerusalem. Now, notice above that the LORD goes out from Zion in Jerusalem to battle against the nations in the Valley of Jehoshaphat. Now, you have seen from Scripture why I say there will be no Battle of Armageddon. The battle will be at Jerusalem.

There is something else on our list that we need to place in sequence regarding the Messiah's Second Coming.

The Wrath of God

When is the Wrath of God completed against the wicked? Once again Scripture has the answer.

> "The LORD will be king over the whole earth. On that day there will be one LORD, and his name the only name.... Jerusalem will be secure. This is the plague with which **the LORD will strike all the nations that fought against Jerusalem**: Their flesh will rot while they are still standing on their feet, their eyes will rot in their sockets, and their tongues will rot in their mouths. On that day men will be stricken by the LORD with great panic. Each man will seize the hand of another, and they will attack each other. ... **Then the survivors from all the nations that have attacked Jerusalem will go up year after year to worship the King, the LORD Almighty, and to celebrate the Feast of Tabernacles**" (Zechariah 14:9-16).

When the final wrath of God is poured out, Yahweh strikes the nations who fought against Jerusalem. This means that after He defeats the armies of the nations in the valley of Jehoshaphat, He will then punish the nations themselves.

Also, notice in last sentence of Zechariah's prophecy. There will be survivors from the nations. The survivors will be those who will repopulate the earth during the thousand years that we call the Millennium. The survivors will be in flesh and blood moral bodies. All those who were Yahweh's people before the Second Coming will be in their resurrected, immortal bodies. Paul touched on this fact in 1 Corinthians 15 when he said,

> "I declare to you, brothers, that flesh and blood cannot inherit the kingdom of God, nor does the perishable inherit the imperishable" (1 Corinthians 15:50).

I'm not going to cover all the details of the Millennium here. For more on that see the Old Testament prophets or my second book, "The Complete Idiot's Guide to the Last Days."

There is something else very important that we need to know. You may have noticed in most of the Old Testament passages regarding the Second Coming that a title was used to identify God. That title was "the LORD."

His Name is Yahweh

There are many titles and adjectives used for the God of the Bible, but He has only one name. The name of God is the name by which He is to be remembered through all generations, just as He said to Moses.

> "God also said to Moses, "Say to the Israelites, 'Yahweh, the God of your fathers--the God of Abraham, the God of Isaac and the God of Jacob--has sent me to you.' This is my name forever, the name by which I am to be remembered from generation to generation" (Exodus 3:15).

As information is rapidly increasing in our electronic world, more and more people are becoming aware of things that were previously hidden or over looked. One of these hidden and overlooked things is the name of the God of the Bible. The truth about the name of God is stranger than fiction.

The people of God, first the Israelites and then the Christians, have systematically hidden the name of Yahweh from the Biblical text. But, today there are many sources which thoroughly address this issue, so I will not attempt to cover that topic here. But for those who would like to dig deeper into this important topic, see the website, **www.hisnameisyahweh.org**.

In short, during the Babylonian captivity of the Israelites around the 6th century BC, the Israelites decided that the name of God was so sacred that it could not be spoken. They believed that merely speaking the name of the Hebrew God was blasphemous and punishable by death. Jewish religious leaders went to great lengths to prevent anyone from blaspheming God's name. They began to remove the name from the text and replaced it with a title.

It is this title, "the LORD" which we, today, find in our English translations.

Everywhere in Scripture that we see "LORD" or "the LORD" written in all capital letters the original Hebrew text records the name of God, "YHWH". "YHWH" is the personal name of God which many believe is pronounced "Yahweh".

Because the name of "YHWH" has not been spoken for centuries, it is very likely that the pronunciation of "Yahweh" is not totally correct.

It's only my intention to point out the obvious. The title "the LORD" is not God's name it is a title given by Man. The Hebrew letters for God's name in English are "YHWH". Therefore, we should be aware of that fact and not continue under some false idea regarding His name.

"Yahweh" is the name of God and "the LORD" is a tile. With that being said, let's see what the Word of God has to say about the importance of God's unique name. God first revealed His personal name to Moses when He sent Moses to the Israelites. Here is how the conversation went:

"Moses said to God, 'Suppose I go to the Israelites and say to them, The God of your fathers has sent me to you,' and they ask me, '**What is his name**?' Then what shall I tell them?' God said to Moses, 'I AM WHO I AM'. This is what you are to say to the Israelites: 'I AM has sent me to you.'" (Exodus 3:13-14)

God's identification of himself as "I AM WHO I AM" comes from the Hebrew word "hayah" which means to exist. "Hayah" used twice is "I AM WHO I AM" in this context means "I eternally exist" or "I am self-existent".

Note: The Hebrew meaning of "I AM WHO I AM" and the name "Yahweh" are the same.

God gave Moses His unique name to be remembered.

The LORD is Yahweh

Following His first declaration, God revealed His personal name to Moses and commanded that His name be remembered forever. Here is what God said:

"God also said to Moses, "Say to the Israelites, 'The LORD [**Yahweh**], the God of your fathers--the God of Abraham, the God of Isaac and the God of Jacob--has sent me to you.' This is my name forever, **the name by which I am to be remembered from generation to generation**." (Exodus 3:15)

God says, His name is Yahweh and that we are to remember His name from generation to generation. His name is to be praised. Did the previous generation tell you the name of Yahweh?

If not, why not? Did someone forget the name Yahweh? Did we forget what Yahweh commanded regarding His name, in the third commandment of the Ten Commandments?

Yahweh's Second Coming

So, as we read about the Second Coming of the Messiah in the Old Testament prophets we were actually reading about the Second Coming of Yahweh. When was Yahweh in Jerusalem that He will return as He says here?

> "Therefore, this is what **Yahweh** (the LORD) says: **'I will return to Jerusalem** with mercy, and there my house will be rebuilt. And the measuring line will be stretched out over Jerusalem,' declares **Yahweh** (the LORD) Almighty" (Zechariah 1:16).

> "This is what **Yahweh** Almighty says: "I am very jealous for Zion; I am burning with jealousy for her. This is what **Yahweh** says: "**I will return to Zion and dwell in Jerusalem.** Then Jerusalem will be called the City of Truth, and the mountain of **Yahweh** Almighty will be called the Holy Mountain" (Zechariah 8:2-3).

The reason that Yahweh can return to Jerusalem is because He was there at His First Coming. When Yahweh returns it will be His Second Coming. Yahweh, the Father, and Yeshua, the Son are one.

Yahweh says,

> "Hear, O Israel: Yahweh our God, Yahweh is one" (Deuteronomy 6:4).

The Messiah says,

> "I and the Father (Yahweh) are one" (John 10:30).

Here is a passage from Jeremiah 23 where Yahweh is talking about the coming Messiah. Yahweh tells us what the name of the Messiah will be when His kingdom comes and He begins to reign on earth from Jerusalem. Here is what Yahweh said,

"The days are coming," **declares Yahweh**, "when I will raise up to David a righteous Branch, a King who will reign wisely and do what is just and right in the land. In his days Judah will be saved and Israel will live in safety. This is the name by which he will be called: **Yahweh** Our Righteousness" (Jeremiah 23:5-6).

We see the same thing over and over in Scripture. Here is another example.

"On that day living water will flow out from Jerusalem, half to the eastern sea and half to the western sea, in summer and in winter. **Yahweh will be king over the whole earth. On that day there will be one Yahweh, and his name the only name**" (Zechariah 14:8-9).

That right, not the name of Jesus, not the name of Yeshua. "On that day there will be one Yahweh, and his name the only name." Yahweh is one!

There is one more thing we should cover in this chapter on the Second Coming before we move on. We have covered the Seven Seal Prophecies and the Seven Trumpet prophecies. Now, we will cover the Seven Bowl Prophecies.

Seven Bowls of Wrath

The Seven Bowl prophecies of Revelation are prophecies about the Wrath of God being poured out on the world, as we see here.

"Then I heard a loud voice from the temple saying to the seven angels, 'Go, pour out the seven bowls of God's wrath on the earth'" (Revelation 16:1).

We should realize that the Wrath of God is poured out on the wicked and unbelieving world beginning when the Messiah returns on the Day of Yahweh. Therefore, as we examine each of the Seven Bowl prophecies we should imagine that they start to be poured out from the time that Messiah appears until His wrath is complete following the final battle at Jerusalem. Let's look at the first five prophecies to see what happens first.

> "**The first** angel went and poured out his bowl on the land, and ugly and painful sores broke out on the people who had the mark of the beast and worshiped his image.
> **The second** angel poured out his bowl on the sea, and it turned into blood like that of a dead man, and every living thing in the sea died.
> **The third** angel poured out his bowl on the rivers and springs of water, and they became blood. Then I heard the angel in charge of the waters say: "You are just in these judgments, you who are and who were, the Holy One, because you have so judged; for they have shed the blood of your saints and prophets, and you have given them blood to drink as they deserve." And I heard the altar respond: "Yes, Lord God Almighty, true and just are your judgments."
> **The fourth** angel poured out his bowl on the sun, and the sun was given power to scorch people with fire. They were seared by the intense heat and they cursed the name of God, who had control over these plagues, but they refused to repent and glorify him"
> **The fifth** angel poured out his bowl on the throne of **the beast, and his kingdom was plunged into darkness**. Men gnawed their tongues in agony and cursed the God of heaven because of their pains and their sores, but they refused to repent of what they had done. (Revelation 16:2-9).

These things are happening to the world at the same time that the Messiah is in Jerusalem with His people. Yahweh's people have been gathered to Him on the Day of Trumpets and then ten days later on the Day of Atonement, He will reward His people for their labor. Then as Yahweh and His people prepare for the Feast of Tabernacles the world is also preparing.

"**The sixth** angel poured out his bowl on the great river
Euphrates, and its water was dried up to prepare the way for
the kings from the East. Then I saw three evil spirits that
looked like frogs; they came out of the mouth of the dragon,
out of the mouth of the beast and out of the mouth of the
false prophet. ... to gather them for the battle on the great
day of God Almighty. ... Then they gathered the kings
together to the place that in Hebrew is called Armageddon"
(Revelation 16:10-16).

From what we can tell, as Yahweh and His people are on Mount
Zion in Jerusalem, the Antichrist and False Prophet are gathering at
Armageddon. They will then come down the Valley of Jehoshaphat
to attack Jerusalem. That is when the Messiah excuses Himself from
the wedding Banquet on Mount Zion to finish some unsettled
business as the prophets declare.

"**Yahweh will roar from Zion** and thunder from Jerusalem;
the earth and the sky will tremble. But Yahweh will be a
refuge for his people, a stronghold for the people of Israel"
(Joel 3:16).

"He said: "**Yahweh roars from Zion** and thunders from
Jerusalem; the pastures of the shepherds dry up, and the top
of Carmel withers." This is what Yahweh says: "For three
sins of Damascus, even for four, **I will not turn back my
wrath**" (Amos 1:2-3).

Then the seventh and last bowl of Yahweh's wrath is poured out.

"The seventh angel poured out his bowl into the air, and out
of the temple came a loud voice from the throne, saying, "It
is done!" (Revelation 16:17).

Then Yahweh and His people will live happily ever after.

What we now know:

- Messiah returns after the Great Tribulation.
- The sun, moon and stars sign precedes the Day of Yahweh.
- At the last trumpet all Yahweh's people will be resurrected.
- The angels will gather Yahweh's people.
- Messiah returns to the Mount of Olives, then Mount Zion.
- Messiah judges and rewards His people.
- Messiah holds the wedding banquet for His people.
- Messiah fights against the kings of the earth and their armies.
- Messiah pours out His wrath on the wicked.
- Yahweh will reside in Jerusalem forever.

Chapter 11
End Time Religion

We have already examined many of the prophecies that describe the biblical "Time of the End" and several that describe the "Day of Yahweh." During our discussions through the Time of the End we have touched on what was happening with Yahweh's people. At the beginning of the Time of the End everyone in the household of God was sound asleep to the fact that the Time had come. However, Yahweh was not going to allow that to continue for very long.

Over the years as I have been reading and studying prophecy about the "Last Days", the "Time of the End" and the Second Coming, Yahweh has given me a picture of the household of God, those that call themselves His Church.

Whether the Church is awake or asleep is critically important. If the Church is asleep it is unable to be alert, on guard and watchful as Christ commanded it to be. Therefore, I felt led to present what Yahweh has revealed to me about End Time Religion and the "Household of God."

Before we begin to discuss End Time Religion, I need to draw a strong contrast between organized religion in God's name and the individuals who will truly comprise the body of Yahweh's people. Not everyone who is in a household of God is one of Yahweh's people.

Yahweh's People

For the purposes of this discussion I will mainly use the term "Yahweh's People" for those individuals whose names are written in the Book of Life and who will inherit the coming Kingdom. While the term "Yahweh's People" or "Yahweh's Family" may be new to many people, it is found in Scripture, as we see below:

> "**Yahweh will establish you as his holy people**, as he promised you on oath, **if you** keep the commands of Yahweh your God and walk in his ways. Then all the peoples on earth will see that **you are called by the name of Yahweh**, and they will fear you" (Deuteronomy 28:9-10).

> "For this reason I kneel before the Father [Yahweh], from whom **his whole family in heaven and on earth derives its name**" (Ephesians 3:14-15).

> "Yahweh said: … if **my people, who are called by my name**, will humble themselves and pray and seek my face and turn from their wicked ways, then will I hear from heaven and will forgive their sin and will heal their land" (2 Chronicles 7:12-14).

According to Christ there are only two types of people in the world; Yahweh's people (the sons of the kingdom) and others (the sons of the evil one). Here is how Christ made that distinction,

> "The one who sowed the good seed is the Son of Man. The field is the world, and the good seed stands for the **sons of the kingdom**. The weeds are the **sons of the evil one**, and the enemy who sows them is the devil. The harvest is the end of the age, and the harvesters are angels. "As the weeds are pulled up and burned in the fire, so it will be at the end of the age. The Son of Man will send out his angels, and they will weed out of his kingdom everything that causes sin and all who do evil. They will throw them into the fiery furnace, where there will be weeping and gnashing of teeth. Then the righteous will shine like the sun in the kingdom of their Father" (Matthew 13:37-43).

Yahweh's people will inherit the Kingdom when it comes, the others will not.

What about the Jewish, Israel and Gentile thing? Here is what the Word of Yahweh says about His people.

> "A man is not a Jew if he is only one outwardly, nor is circumcision merely outward and physical. No, **a man is a Jew if he is one inwardly; and circumcision is circumcision of the heart, by the Spirit**, not by the written code. Such a man's praise is not from men, but from God" (Romans 2:28-29).

> "This mystery is that through the gospel **the Gentiles are heirs together with Israel, members together of one body**, and sharers together in the promise in Christ Jesus" (Ephesians 3:6).

> "For not all who are descended from Israel are Israel. ... In other words, **it is not the natural children who are God's children**, but it is the children of the promise who are regarded as Abraham's offspring" (Romans 9:6-8).

Israel and Gentiles, in the faith, are one body and joint heirs of the Kingdom. Israel and the Gentiles in the Messiah are "Yahweh's People."

Household of God

> "God's household, which is the church of the living God, the pillar and foundation of the truth" (1 Timothy 3:15).

The household of God is the local fellowship, the religious denomination or the church organization that professes to follow the God of the Bible. It is possible that there are "sons of the kingdom" in many of these religious organizations. However, not all members of these religious organizations are "Yahweh's people." Not all leaders of these groups are "Yahweh's people." Only, Yahweh knows who are His and who are not. Not even the angels in heaven know who's for real.

Today, almost 2,000 years after the Messiah's First Coming, there are more Bible based religious groups than can be counted. These thousands and thousands of religious organizations use all kinds of teachings and traditions in their worship and religious practices. After 2,000 years all these groups, virtually every one, has added to or taken away from the biblical teachings of Yahweh. Some of the teachings and traditions in the 'Household of God" even have pagan origins like; Christmas, Easter and Sunday worship to mention just a few. Some are just things that people have made up.

These teachings and traditions in the so called Bible based religions make it almost impossible for its leaders and members to see the Truth in Scripture. I know this is a hard thing to accept, but it is apparent in Scripture and discernable in the Spirit.

Let's examine "End Time Religion."

As we begin to examine End Time Religion we will find that Scripture has almost nothing good to say about the state and condition of the Household of God and its leadership.

Religion that Yahweh accepts

For perspective, here is what Yahweh accepts as religion.

> **"Religion that God our Father accepts as pure and faultless is this**: to look after orphans and widows in their distress and to keep oneself from being polluted by the world" (James 1:27).

Scripture indicates that Yahweh does not change which means He has not and will not come up with a new form of religion. Here is what Yahweh said originally about worshiping Him. When speaking to the Israelites about their exposure to other forms of worship, Yahweh said this,

> **"You must not worship Yahweh your God in their way,** because in worshiping their gods, they do all kinds of detestable things Yahweh hates. They even burn their sons and daughters in the fire as sacrifices to their gods. **See that you do all I command you; do not add to it or take away from it"** (Deuteronomy 12:31-32).

This is what the Father said. Yahweh instructs His people to worship Him His way without adding to it or taking away from it. This is the will of the Father.

Now, here is what Christ said about the will of the Father.

> **"Not everyone** who says to me, 'Lord, Lord,' **will enter the kingdom** of heaven, **but only he who does the will of my Father** who is in heaven. Many will say to me on that day, 'Lord, Lord, did we not prophesy in your name, and in your name drive out demons and perform many miracles?' Then I will tell them plainly, 'I never knew you. Away from me, you who break the law!" (Matthew 7:21-23).

Yahweh gave us the law, the Messiah says to do it and Paul confirmed what Yahweh said.

But, some people say Paul changed all that. What does Paul say? First, here is what Peter said about Paul's writings:

> **"Paul also wrote you with the wisdom that God gave him**. ... His letters contain some things that are hard to understand, **which ignorant and unstable people distort, as they do the other Scriptures, to their own destruction"** (2 Peter 3:15).

Not everything that Paul wrote was hard to understand. Some things were profoundly straight forward and clear. For example, in this passage Paul's agreement with Yahweh and Christ is emphatically clear.

> "Is God the God of Jews only? Is he not the God of Gentiles too? Yes, of Gentiles too, since there is only one God, who will justify the circumcised **by faith** and the uncircumcised through that **same faith. Do we, then, nullify the law by this faith? Not at all! Rather, we uphold the law**" (Romans 3:29-31).

I'm not going to belabor the point. However, I know of no religious groups who uphold the law with out adding to it or taking away from it. Now, if I am wrong, I would love to meet such a group. But, before you jump to conclusions, do your biblical homework. Forget what man says and know what Yahweh says. His Word is truth! Man's opinion, not so much!

At the time of the Messiah's First Coming, He warned His people about the Time of the End and left them with specific instructions.

Christ's End Time Instructions

Let's review a few of Christ's instruction to His people, as we prepare for our discussion of End Time Religion. Christ said,

> "Be on guard! Be alert! You do not know when that time will come.... Therefore keep watch ... If he comes suddenly, **do not let him find you sleeping.** What I say to you, I say to everyone: 'Watch!'" (Mark 13:33-37)

Christ reiterated His warning many times including here in Revelation.

> "Remember, therefore, what you have received and heard; obey it, and repent. But **if you do not wake up**, I will come like a thief, and you will not know at what time I will come to you" (Revelation 3:3).

"Behold, I come like a thief! **Blessed is he who stays awake**" (Revelation 16:15).

Clearly, Christ wanted His people to stay awake! However, He also knew that they would not be awake when the Time of the End arrived. Christ used various ways to emphasize the seriousness of His warning, as we have seen. In the same context of being awake, He also told us,

> "**Be on guard! Be alert!** You do not know when that time will come.... **Therefore keep watch** ... If he comes suddenly, do not let him find you sleeping. What I say to you, I say to everyone: **'Watch!'**" (Mark 13:33-37)

Each of these; being on guard, being alert and keeping watch are all related to being awake. If Yahweh's people are asleep then they will be unable to follow these other instructions.

Christ has already told us, in prophecy, everything about the Time of the End. He expects us to know what He has told us ahead of time, so that we will be able to recognize the signs when they appear. Here are a couple of things He said, that communicate that idea.

> "**Be on your guard. I have told you everything ahead of time**" (Mark 13:23).

> "Even so, **when you see** all these things, **you know that it is near**, right at the door" Matthew 24:33).

However, Christ already knew that His people would be asleep and not realize that the Time of the End had already come when He opened the First Seal on 9/11 in 2001.

First of all, immediately after 9/11 it was estimated that over half of all Americans went to church.

What happened in the churches after 9/11, when the First Seal opened?

The churches began to pray and seek God about what had happen. They sought Him in prayer. However, they did not seek Him in His Word in spite of the fact that He had "already told them everything ahead of time." In short, the churches did not seek Yahweh, His way and therefore He was not going to listen.

This situation between Yahweh and His people is well described in the prophecies of Jeremiah. Yahweh's people prayed, but they did not listen to Him, His Word was offensive to them. I suggest that you read the whole thing in context. However, for our purposes, let's just look at a few excerpts.

> "To whom can I speak and give warning? **Who will listen to me?** Their ears are closed so they cannot hear. **The word of Yahweh is offensive to them;** they find no pleasure in it. **But I am full of the wrath of Yahweh, and I cannot hold it in**" (Jeremiah 6:10-11).

> "This is what Yahweh says: 'Stand at the crossroads and look; **ask for the ancient paths, ask where the good way is, and walk in it,** and you will find rest for your souls. But you said, **'We will not walk in it.'** I appointed watchmen over you and said, 'Listen to the sound of the trumpet!' **But you said, 'We will not listen.'** Therefore hear, O nations; observe, O witnesses, what will happen to them" (Jeremiah 6:16-18).

When Yahweh opens the Second Seal, we'll get a sense of His anger with His people and His household. Yahweh also explains why He did not listen to His people when they prayed following 9/11.

> "They have returned to the sins of their forefathers, who **refused to listen to my words.** They have followed other gods to serve them. Both the house of Israel and the house of Judah have broken the covenant I made with their forefathers. **Therefore this is what Yahweh says: 'I will bring on them a disaster** they cannot escape. Although they cry out to me, **I will not listen to them**" (Jeremiah 11:19/11).

In spite of their disobedience, Yahweh will not allow His people to remain asleep. He planned to wake them from their sleep before it's too late. The 9/11 birth pain was not big enough to awaken the Household of God. So, the Second Seal birth pain will be **much bigger.** When the Second Seal is opened all of Yahweh's households and all of Yahweh's people will awake in shock. Nothing in Yahweh's household or in the world will ever be the same again.

The world will not be able to understand what is happening. However, if Yahweh's people will do what Scripture says, they will know what to do.

> "My son, **keep your father's commands and do not forsake the law.** Bind them upon your heart forever; fasten them around your neck. When you walk, they (commands and the law) will guide you; when you sleep, they (commands and the law) will watch over you; **when you awake, they (commands and the law) will speak to you.** For these commands are a lamp, this teaching is a light, and the corrections of discipline are the way to life" (Proverbs 6:20-23).

When this happens, Yahweh will be correcting His people for wondering away from His commands and law, turning from His ways. However, those who He left in charge of His household will be held to a higher standard.

> "**Not many of you should presume to be teachers**, my brothers, because you know that we who teach will be judged more strictly" (James 3:1).

> "**You also must be ready**, because the Son of Man will come at an hour when you do not expect him. ... That servant who knows his master's will and does not get ready or does not do what his master wants will be beaten with many blows. ... From everyone who has been given much, **much will be demanded**" (Luke 12:40, 47-48).

Christ warned the pastors that there would be dire consequences if they failed to follow His instructions.

Prophecy at the Proper Time

Here is an excerpt from Christ's warning to the pastors,

> "If the owner of the house had known at what time of night the thief was coming, he would have kept watch and would not have let his house be broken into. ... Who then is the faithful and wise servant, **whom the master has put in charge of** the servants in **his household to give them their food at the proper time?** ... But suppose that servant is wicked and says to himself, 'My master is staying away a long time,' ... The master of that servant will come on a day when he does not expect him and ... cut him to pieces and assign him a place with the hypocrites, where there will be weeping and gnashing of teeth" (Matthew 24:43-51).

The "food at the proper time" is prophecy concerning the Time of the End. The reason I differentiate prophecy about the End Time from other Scripture is due to the context of Matthew 24 and 25 which is about the Time of the End.

"Jesus answered, "It is written: 'Man does not live on bread alone, but on **every word that comes from the mouth of God**'" (Matthew 3:4).

Isaiah was also told that **all the End Time Shepherds** would be caught off guard, in spite of Yahweh's repeated warnings.

"**Israel's watchmen are blind, they all lack knowledge**; they are all mute dogs, they cannot bark; they lie around and dream, they love to sleep. … **They are shepherds who lack understanding**; **they all** turn to their own way, each seeks his own gain" (Isaiah 56:10-11).

Yahweh is not pleased with these shepherds. Here is what He said through Ezekiel,

"This is what the Sovereign Yahweh says**: I am against the shepherds** and will hold them accountable for my flock. **I will remove them from tending the flock so that the shepherds can no longer feed themselves**. I will rescue my flock from their mouths, and it will no longer be food for them. … I myself will search for my sheep and look after them" (Ezekiel 34:10-11).

There will be serious consequences for the shepherds as well as the flock for not staying wake and being alert to the Time of the End. All God's people should have been in their Bibles, reading about the Second Coming and keeping watch. If they had, they would have been awake and able to identify Revelation's First Seal prophecy years earlier.

Never the less, God knew this would happen. That is why He planned that they would all wake up when He opened the Second Seal. At the Second Seal there will still be time! But, no time to lose!

More than Prophecy

Prophecy is not the only thing that the pastors and people in God's Household had forgotten! From the beginning Yahweh had warned His people to remember the main things, those things that Yahweh held high.

> "I will bow down toward your holy temple and will praise your name for your love and your faithfulness, **for you have exalted above all things your name and your word**" (psalm 138:2).

Today, many of Yahweh's people have forgotten His name and even fewer know what He says. For example, do you know that the commandments and law of Yahweh are eternal?

> **"All your words are true; all your righteous laws are eternal"** (Psalm 119:160).

Eternal means existing at all times without change.

The sad state of affairs is that, today most Christians do not know nor understand the third and fourth commandments of the Ten Commandments. The Commandments, which Yahweh Himself wrote in stone by His own finger. Wow! Talk about written in stone!

> "When Yahweh finished speaking to Moses on Mount Sinai, he gave him the two tablets of the Testimony, the **tablets of stone inscribed by the finger of God**" (Exodus 31:18).

What does Yahweh say when His people and their leaders forget about the things that He told them to remember and do from generation to generation?

Yahweh told us ahead of Time!

Yahweh here is telling Jeremiah how things will be with Yahweh's people in the Time of the End. For example, this could be written to Christians who live in the USA during the time between the Second and Third Seals of Revelation.

"From the least to the greatest, all are greedy for gain; prophets and priests alike, all practice deceit. … Yahweh says: 'Stand at the crossroads and look; ask for the ancient paths, ask where the good way is, and walk in it, and you will find rest for your souls. But you said, **'We will not walk in it.' I appointed watchmen over you and said, 'Listen** to the sound of the trumpet!' But you said, **'We will not listen.'** Therefore hear, O nations; observe, O witnesses, what will happen to them. Hear, O earth: I am bringing disaster on this people, the fruit of their schemes, <u>because</u> **they have not listened to my words and have rejected my law**" (Jeremiah 6:13-19).

The prophet Hosea captured the condition that Yahweh's people would be in when the Time of the End came. Here is what Hosea wrote. The first verse is familiar to many Christians, but they fail to grasp it in its context. See if you can see what I mean.

"my people are destroyed from lack of knowledge. "Because you have rejected knowledge, I also reject you as my priests; **because you have ignored the law of your God,** I also will ignore your children. The more **the priests** increased, the more they **sinned against me**; they exchanged their Glory for something disgraceful. They feed on the sins of my people and relish their wickedness. And **it will be: Like people, like priests**" (Hosea 4:6-9).

"Like people, like priests" means the priests are teaching what the people want to hear. The people are leading the priests. It should be the other way around. However, by the Time of the End the "household of Yahweh" will be teaching what is popular, Not the eternal Word of Yahweh. The New Testament contains the same message regarding the "Household of Yahweh." For example:

"For the time will come when **men will not put up with sound doctrine**. Instead, to suit their own desires, **they will gather around them a great number of teachers to say what their itching ears want to hear**. They will turn their ears away from the truth and turn aside to myths" (2 Timothy 4:3-4).

Teachers should teach and lead men, not the other way around. Once again in the Time of the End teachers will be teaching what's popular, not what Yahweh says. Here is an example,

Many of today's teachers say that there will be a Pre-Tribulation Rapture even though this teaching cannot be found in Scripture.

Christ clearly stated this, about His return to gather His people.

"Immediately **after the tribulation** … They will see the Son of Man [**Messiah**] **coming on the clouds of the sky**, with power and great glory. And he will send his angels **with a loud trumpet call, and they will gather his elect**" (Matthew 24:29-31).

So, if the shepherds and priests of Yahweh's people fail to follow Yahweh's commands and persist in the teachings and traditions of Man in order to be popular, what does Yahweh say He will do?

Yahweh's against the shepherds.

When Christ told the shepherds to give His people the Word at the proper time, He also warned them about what would happen if they didn't.

"The master of that servant will come on a day when he does not expect him and … **cut him to pieces** and **assign him a place with the hypocrites, where there will be weeping and gnashing of teeth**" (Matthew 24:43-51).

To be assigned a place with hypocrites, where there will be weeping and gnashing of teeth, is the place for unbelievers.

When Yahweh was speaking to Ezekiel about the Time of the End, Yahweh told him what would happen to the disobedient Shepherds, when He said,

> "**I am against the shepherds** and will hold them accountable for my flock. **I will remove them from tending the flock so that the shepherds can no longer feed themselves.** I will rescue my flock from their mouths, and it will no longer be food for them. … I myself will look after them" (Ezekiel 34:10-11).

Yahweh also spoke to Jeremiah about how He would hold the shepherds accountable when He said,

> "**Woe to the shepherds** who are destroying and scattering the sheep of my pasture!" declares Yahweh. Therefore this is what Yahweh, the God of Israel, says to the shepherds who tend my people: "Because you have scattered my flock and driven them away and have not bestowed care on them, **I will bestow punishment on you** for the evil you have done" (Jeremiah 23:1-2).

To lead the flock in ways other than the commandments and the law of Yahweh is to scatter the flock from their pasture. Because the shepherds have turned from the eternal ways of Yahweh to the teachings and traditions of Man, Yahweh will punish them. They will be punished during the Time of the End as well as their eternal punishment on Judgment Day (The Day of Yahweh).

> "Both prophet and priest are godless; even in my temple I find their wickedness," declares Yahweh. Therefore **their path will become slippery; they will be banished to darkness and there they will fall. I will bring disaster on them in the year they are punished**," declares Yahweh" (Jeremiah 23:11-12).

"**The shepherds will have nowhere to flee,** the leaders of the flock no place to escape. **Hear the cry of the shepherds, the wailing of the leaders of the flock, for Yahweh is destroying their pasture.** The peaceful meadows will be laid waste because of the fierce anger of Yahweh" (Jeremiah 25:35-36).

Yahweh is very angry at the shepherds of His flock because they did not lead the people on the ancient paths but scattered them. Notice that this prophecy is from Jeremiah 50 which is about the End Time Babylonians. The shepherds in the USA have led Yahweh's people astray and their punishment will be severe.

"My people have been lost sheep; their shepherds have led them astray and caused them to roam on the mountains. They wandered over mountain and hill and forgot their own resting place. Whoever found them devoured them" (Jeremiah 50:6-7).

Not only is there punishment for the shepherds in End Time Babylon but also the false prophets. Never the less, Yahweh will shepherd and guide His people **to His land for their rest.** Here is how Yahweh describes this Time of the End in the land of the Babylonians.

"Yet their Redeemer is strong; Yahweh Almighty is his name. He will vigorously defend their cause so that he may bring **rest to their land**, but unrest to those who live in Babylon. A sword against the Babylonians!" declares Yahweh -- "against those who live in Babylon and **against her officials and wise men! A sword against her false prophets!**" (Jeremiah 50:34-36).

Yahweh's Anger against the shepherds and false prophets of His flock during the Time of the End is very well documented in prophecy. I encourage all Yahweh's people to read Ezekiel 34, one of the most descriptive discourses regarding the End Time Shepherds. Ezekiel 34 also explains where Yahweh's people are to turn when they wake up and realize that they need a new shepherd.

Zechariah received a similar message about the End Time Shepherds.

> "The idols speak deceit, diviners see visions that lie; they tell dreams that are false, they give comfort in vain. Therefore the people wander like sheep oppressed **for lack of a shepherd**. My anger burns against the shepherds, and I will punish the leaders; for **Yahweh Almighty will care for his flock**" (Zechariah 10:2-3).

Yahweh's against the prophets.

Yahweh also spoke extensively about the false prophets in the Time of the End. In Jeremiah and Ezekiel, Yahweh expresses His anger. The false prophets have miss used His word, claiming things in His name, that He did not say. Yahweh was also angry that these End Time Prophets thought more of the popular teachings of Man than they did of Yahweh's Word. These prophecies in Jeremiah 23 and Ezekiel 13 are very descriptive and I strongly suggest that you read and meditate on what Yahweh is revealing in them.

Here are a couple of short passages so you can get an idea of what Yahweh is saying about these false prophets.

> "This is what Yahweh Almighty says: "**Do not listen to what the prophets are prophesying to you**; they fill you with **false hopes**. They speak visions from their own minds, not from the mouth of Yahweh. They keep saying to those who despise me, ' Yahweh says: **You will have peace**.' And to all who follow the stubbornness of their hearts they say, **'No harm will come to you.**' But which of them has stood in the council of Yahweh to <u>see</u> **or to hear his word**? Who has **listened and heard his word**? See, the storm of Yahweh will burst out in wrath, a whirlwind swirling down on the heads of the wicked" (Jeremiah 23:16-19).

What "false hopes" is Yahweh speaking of? Could He be referring to the false hope of a Pre-Tribulation Rapture? When Yahweh says that the false prophets tell His people "No harm will come to you", could this also be talking about the Pre-Tribulation Rapture? Or could it be about the false hope that says, "Once saved always saved"? Of course this once saved always saved teaching could only be true if it said this, "Once saved always saved, if saved at the End."

You can see why Yahweh is very angry at the false prophets of the Time of the End. Because they are leading His people astray! That is why He says,

> "Son of man, **prophesy against the prophets of Israel** who are now prophesying. Say to those who prophesy out of **their own imagination**: 'Hear the word of Yahweh! This is what the Sovereign Yahweh says: Woe to **the foolish prophets** who **follow their own spirit and have seen nothing!**" (Ezekiel 13:2-3).

> "**Their visions are false** and their divinations a lie. They say, "Yahweh declares," when Yahweh has not sent them; yet **they expect their words to be fulfilled.** Have you not seen false visions and uttered lying divinations when you say, "Yahweh declares," **though I have not spoken?**" (Ezekiel 13:6-7).

Notice, that Yahweh is telling us that these false prophets are themselves deceived. They expect their lies to be fulfilled. In other words, the false prophets are sincere, sincerely deceived. However, the main idea is that they have not heard from Yahweh nor seen in His Word what they are proclaiming. This speaks about the "Pre-Tribulation Rapture" lie, because it is something that cannot be found in Scripture.

This is another good example of why Yahweh's people must rely on Yahweh and His Word, as led by His Spirit. We each must seek Yahweh personally because anything else causes us to trust in Man and that is not an option in the Time of the End. Yahweh is our Shepherd and we must take refuge in Him alone.

"It is better to take refuge in Yahweh than to trust in man.
It is better to take refuge in Yahweh than to trust in princes"
(Psalm 118:8-9).

"This is what Yahweh says: "**Cursed is the one who trusts in man,** who depends on flesh for his strength and **whose heart turns away from Yahweh**"
(Jeremiah 17:5).

The Time of the End Has Come, Turn to Yahweh in Obedience!

Glossary of Terms

Each term will include synonyms followed by a definition and a reference verse and a statement if the term is **not** biblical.

Abomination that causes Desolation:

Is when the Antichrist goes into the Temple of God and proclaims himself to be God. This act of blasphemy starts the Great Tribulation. Daniel 9:27

Abyss:

The Abyss is the place located in the earth where Yahweh holds demons until the appointed time. Satan will be locked and sealed in the Abyss at the Messiah's return and remain there for thousand years. Revelation 9:1-2

Antichrist: beast, ruler who will come, man of lawlessness

The world ruler who will rise to power out of the fourth beast kingdom, Daniel 7:23-24. During the Great Tribulation he will receive power from Satan to deceive the world and destroy the people of Yahweh. 1 John 2:18

Ark of the Covenant:

The Gold covered wooden chest which contained the Ten Commandments. Exodus 25:10-22

Armageddon:

Where the Antichrist will gather the kings of the earth and their armies in preparation for of the great battle against Jerusalem. Revelation 16:16.
There will be no battle at the place called Armageddon.

Babylon the Great, Mystery: Land of the Babylonians

The End Time Superpower which holds a position of great influence over the world until she is destroyed by the Fourth Beast Kingdom of the Antichrist. Revelation 17-18

Bible: Scripture, Word of God, Word of Truth

Yahweh's inspired written Word. Includes the Old Testament, containing 39 books which was written before the First Coming of the Messiah and the New Testament, containing 27 books which was written following His First Coming. 2 Timothy 2:15

Birth Pains:

A prophetic term used by the Messiah and the Old Testament Prophets to describe events which will take place on earth before the coming of the Kingdom of God. The beginning birth pains, like the first four Seals of Revelation, are early warning signs to the return of the Messiah. Matthew 24:8

Beast, The: Antichrist, man of lawlessness

The End Time world ruler from the Middle East who will receive power from Satan, Revelation 13:3, and attempt to destroy the people of God. Revelation 13:5

Beast Kingdom, The Fourth:

This Middle-eastern kingdom will rise to world power during the Time of the End. The Antichrist will arise from within this kingdom and overthrow three of its ten kings. Daniel 7:24

Believers: Saints, elect, Christians, Church, Body of the Messiah

Everyone, throughout history who has put their faith in Yahweh. Everyone, whose name is written in the Book of Life. John 4:41

Book of Life:

> Yahweh's record of everyone who has put their faith in Him. Psalm 69:28

Children of the Resurrection:

> A title Jesus gave to His followers, those who will take part in the resurrection and spend their eternal life in the Kingdom with the Messiah. Luke 20:36

Christ: Messiah, Anointed One, Son of God

> The Anointed One, the Messiah, who will return and establish the Kingdom of Yahweh on earth. John 1:41

Devil: Satan, the Dragon

> A powerful angel who rebelled against Yahweh and strives to rise to the throne of Yahweh by destroying Yahweh's people and plans. He will be thrown from heaven to earth by the Archangel Michael at the beginning of the Great Tribulation. Revelation 12:9

Daniel's 70th Week:

> This non-biblical term refers to the last seven years of Daniel's "Seventy 'sevens'" prophecy. To date 483 years of this 490-year prophecy have been fulfilled. One seven-year period is still outstanding and will be fulfilled during the Time of the End. Daniel 9:24-27

Day of the LORD: Day of Yahweh, Day of Wrath, Day of Salvation

The day when the Messiah returns, gathers His elect, punishes the unbelieving world and establishes His Kingdom on earth. That Day is a very significant event in Yahweh's plan. It is referred to by name 24 times in Scripture and written about so often simply referred to it as "the day" or "that day." Several times in Scripture it is called "the great and dreadful day" because it will be a day of deliverance and a day of judgment. Isaiah 13:6

Elementary teachings about the Messiah: elementary truths of Yahweh's Word, Spiritual Milk and the Foundation

The elementary teachings about the Messiah include six doctrinal teachings which are foundational to the Christian faith. They are listed as repentance from acts that lead to death, faith in God, instruction about baptisms, laying on of hands, resurrection of the dead, and eternal judgment. Hebrew 6:1-2

End of the Age:

A term Yeshua used to refer to the time of the harvest and His return, when He will gather His elect and judge the world. Matthew 24:3

False Prophet:

The second beast of Revelation 13 who comes out of the earth and deceives the whole world by performing miraculous signs and causing the inhabitants of the earth to worship the first beast. He and the first beast are destroyed and thrown into the lake of fire at the end of the Great Tribulation. Revelation 16:13

Final Battle: Battle on the Great Day

Non-biblical term for the battle in the Valley of Jehoshaphat on the Day of the LORD. The Antichrist and his forces will gather at Armageddon 70 miles north of Jerusalem and then come down to attack Jerusalem. The Messiah and His supernatural army will slaughter the armies of the Antichrist. Revelation 16:14

Fourth Beast Kingdom:

The Kingdom of the Antichrist which will have 7 leaders and 10 nations which is called the kingdom with "seven heads and ten horns" Daniel 7:23-25.

Gospel:

The Yahweh's message regarding His purpose and plan for His people. Matthew 24:14

Great Tribulation:

The last 3.5 years of this age. A time of trial and testing that will come upon the whole world. Matthew 24:21

Harvest, The:

The gathering of Yahweh's followers into the Kingdom at the end of the age and separating out of all who causes sin and do evil. Matthew 13:39

Judgment Seat of Christ:

The judgment and rewarding of believers, at the Messiah return. 2 Corinthians 5:10

Kingdom of God: Kingdom of Yahweh

The Kingdom on earth, ruled by the Messiah and His followers for 1,000 years. Matthew 12:28

Last Days:

> The period of 3,000 years; two 1,000 year days from the time
> of the Messiah's First Coming and then finally His 1,000
> year day and reign on earth. 2 Peter 3:3

Lord's Day: Seventh Day, Sabbath, Sabbath-rest

> The Lord's Day is recorded in Isaiah 58:13 as the Sabbath,
> the Lord's Holy Day. The Lord's Day is the 7th day Sabbath.
> Hebrews 4:9

Man of lawlessness: Antichrist, beast

> The ruler of the final Middle-eastern kingdom and ruler of
> the world, who proclaims himself to be God. 2 Thessalonians
> 2:3

Mark of the Beast:

> A mark on the right hand or forehead, signifying allegiance
> to the first beast of Revelation 13. The mark allows its wearer
> to buy and sell during the Great Tribulation. Anyone taking
> this mark will be subject to Yahweh's eternal wrath.
> Revelation 16:2

Messiah: Christ, Son of David, Branch, Anointed One

> The King of Yahweh's coming eternal Kingdom on earth
> also know as "Yahweh Our Righteousness". John 1:41 and
> Jeremiah 23:5-6

Michael the Archangel:

> The archangel who protects the people of God, Daniel 12:1
> and who in the last days will battle Satan and throw him to
> earth in the middle of the last seven years. Revelation 12:7

Millennium:

The non-biblical term for the thousand-year reign of the Messiah on earth. Revelation 20:2-7

Prophecy:

Prophecy is Yahweh foretelling the future. Prophecy is history written in advance. Daniel 9:24

Prophet:

A prophet is a person who proclaims a message from God by divine guidance about things which will take place in the future. Exodus 7:1

Rapture: catching up, resurrection of the living

A non-biblical term used to describe the "catching up" from the earth into the clouds of believers who are left alive until the Second Coming. 1 Thessalonians 4:16-17

Rebellion, The: Falling Away, the Apostasy

A turning away from faith which will take place during the Great Tribulation. 2 Thessalonians 2:3

Restrainer, The: Michael the Archangel

Michael, the Great Prince who protects the people of God by restraining Satan. Satan will attempt to kill all God's people during the Great Tribulation, when he is no longer held back. 2 Thessalonians 2:7

Resurrection, First: resurrection of believers

The change which will take place in Yahweh's people, both the dead and the living, at the Messiah's return. Revelation 20:5

Resurrection, Second:

A non-biblical term for the raising of the rest of the dead at the end of the thousand year reign of the Messiah. Revelation 20:5

Revelation, The Book of:

The last book in the Bible. The Messiah's final Word to His followers regarding what will take place during the Time of the End.

Satan: the devil, the great dragon

A powerful angel who rebelled against Yahweh and strives to rise to the throne of Yahweh, by destroying the people and plans of Yahweh. He will be thrown to earth by Archangel Michael at the time of the abomination that causes desolation. Satan will give his power to the Antichrist during the Great Tribulation. He will be bound in the Abyss for a thousand years. Revelation 12:9

Scripture: Bible, Word of God, Word of Truth

The inspired written Word of Yahweh. Mark 12:10

Second Coming: Second Advent, return of the Messiah

The Messiah's return from heaven to earth.

Temple of God: House of God

The "House of God" and the place of Jewish worship in Jerusalem. Solomon built the first temple. The second temple was rebuilt during the time of Nehemiah and was being remodeled by king Herod at the time of the First Coming. Herod's completed temple was destroyed in 70 AD by Syrian troops from Titus's army. There will be a third temple built during the Time of the End. Revelation 11:1

Ten Commandments: Law, Statues

Yahweh's top ten eternal commandments for His people.
Exodus 34:28

Time of the End: End Time

A time of less than 40 years, starting with the opening of the
first seal of Revelation and continuing until the Second
Coming of the Messiah. Daniel 12:9
There are no End Times, there will be only one End Time.

Trumpet, Last:

The seventh trumpet of Revelation 11:15, which will signal
the resurrection of the living and the dead in Christ. 1
Corinthians 15:51-52

Tribulation, Great: time of Jacob's trouble

The 3.5 years of unparalleled persecution and suffering
brought on by Satan through the Antichrist and False
Prophet. It's identified as: 42 months, 1,260 days, and a time,
times and half a time. This period begins with the
"abomination that causes desolation" and ends with the
return of the Messiah. Matthew 24:21

White Throne Judgment, Great:

The final judgment will take place after the thousand-year
earthly reign of the Messiah. The White Throne Judgment is
the judgment of everyone who did not take part in the First
Resurrection. Revelation 20:11

Wedding Banquet: wedding feast, wedding supper

The celebration of the union between Yeshua the Messiah and the Bride of the Messiah (Yahweh's people). It will take place on Mount Zion in Jerusalem. Matthew 25:10 and is described in Isaiah 25:6-8.

Word of God: Bible, Scripture, Word, Word of Truth

Yahweh's inspired written communication to His people, about His purpose and plan. Proverbs 30:5

Wrath of God:

Yahweh's punishment of the unbelieving and disobedient world. It will be poured out on the Day of the LORD. Revelation 19:15

Richard H. Perry

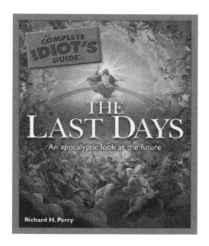

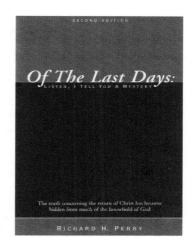

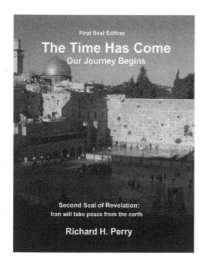

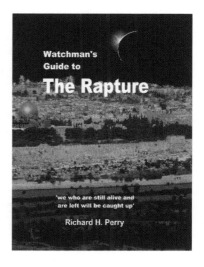

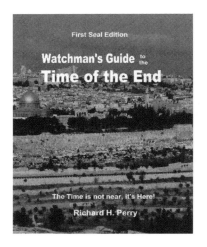

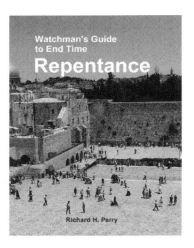

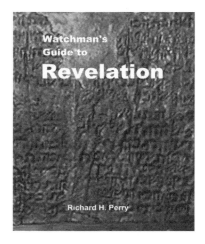

26481305R00113

Made in the USA
Charleston, SC
08 February 2014